EDUCATION
AND THE
SPIRIT OF THE AGE

EDUCATION
AND THE
SPIRIT OF THE AGE

BY

SIR R. W. LIVINGSTONE

SOMETIME PRESIDENT OF
CORPUS CHRISTI COLLEGE
OXFORD

OXFORD
AT THE CLARENDON PRESS
1952

Oxford University Press, Amen House, London E.C. 4
GLASGOW NEW YORK TORONTO MELBOURNE WELLINGTON
BOMBAY CALCUTTA MADRAS CAPE TOWN
Geoffrey Cumberlege, Publisher to the University

PRINTED IN GREAT BRITAIN

PREFACE

THE origin of this book was an invitation to lecture under the Chancellor Dunning Trust at Queen's University, Kingston, Canada, and it embodies the lectures given there in 1950, and at Princeton University on the Vanuxem Foundation. It will always be associated in my mind with the kindness of President Wallace of Queen's and of President Dodds of Princeton and with the generous friendliness of my audiences and of many others in Canada and America.

The book has two main theses. Chapters II to V deal with the need for a philosophy of life; Chapters VI and VII suggest that the analytic attitude and method which dominates modern thinking will give us a very imperfect philosophy, unless it is supplemented by what Shelley in the words quoted on p. 113 calls the creative or poetical faculty. An attempt is made to indicate some educational implications of these views.

I should like to express my gratitude to Mr. W. F. R. Hardie for some criticisms on the chapter on Aristotle and to Mr. Basil Blackwell for allowing me to use the late Mr. H. Rackham's *Aristotle's Ethics for English Readers* for the translations in the same chapter.

R. W. L.

OXFORD

1952

CONTENTS

I

INTRODUCTION

TWO forces remould our educational systems. From within, the restless human intelligence is fitfully at work, correcting their irrationalities, devising better ways of achieving their ends. More powerfully, from without, the changing circumstances of life press upon them, modifying them to meet new conditions, developing new activities, introducing new subjects. Thus in the last hundred years the growth of democracy has transformed education from the privilege of a few to the right of all. 'We must educate our masters', said Lowe in 1867, and, incidentally, our masters decided that they wished to be educated, and a nation-wide system first of primary, then of secondary schools came into existence. Circumstances had, almost automatically, created it. It was circumstances again that forced science and modern languages on education. There was no Honour School of Science in Oxford till 1850, or of Modern Languages till 1903. Rather late in the day it had become apparent that national ignorance of the languages and thoughts of the peoples of the continent was undesirable, and also that serious attention should be paid to the force which was transforming civilization and on which our material prosperity depended; and the two subjects got a firm foothold in the university.

But it is dangerous to consign educational change

entirely to circumstances and to rely on their pressure to do all that is required. Men do, no doubt, see the obvious demands, the superficial suggestions, of a new situation and respond to them. They realize, for instance, that they need a knowledge of Spanish to sell goods in South America, and that science makes it possible to live more comfortably and trade more successfully. So provision is made for the study of Spanish and of science and technology in universities and elsewhere: the immediate claims of new forces moving in the world are met. But the deeper and, ultimately, more important effects of these forces may be overlooked.

How little men may foresee these deeper effects can be illustrated from one of the most momentous changes in the history of Europe, the Renaissance. In the fourteenth century men began to discover a world very unlike their own, 'a new conception of life, freer, larger, more rational, and more joyous, than the medieval; one which gave unfettered scope to the play of the human feelings, to the sense of beauty, and to all the activities of the intellect.'[1] The records of this world were in classical literature. A new star—or rather a star long eclipsed—had risen over the horizon, and its discoverers responded to the vision. They collected manuscripts of the Latin and Greek writers which told them more about it; they interpreted, translated, edited, and later, printed these. But the long-term results of the rediscovery of antiquity were not foreseen. The fourteenth-century Italians never guessed that this new vision of life would by degrees undermine the

[1] *Cambridge Modern History*, i. 538.

ideas and civilization of the Middle Ages, that they were taking the first steps on a road which led to the twentieth century. There were meanings hidden in the word 'humanism' which those who first used it never suspected.

May not something similar be happening to us? Such forces as liberalism, rationalism, and science not only change our social order but also insensibly alter the very texture of our thought, the attitude of our minds, with influences that escape notice because they work below the surface and out of sight. And may not this have bad as well as good results?

It is with this thought in mind that this book has been written—to consider some of the deeper problems which these have set us—not in the material world but in our inner lives, and therefore in education. The field is enormous; I am only raising a few questions in a corner of it, and asking rather than answering these. My excuse is that the matter needs more consideration than perhaps it gets. If the human body is exposed to changed conditions of living, to unfamiliar climate or strange food, we study the results so that we can adjust ourselves and avoid ill consequences to our health. So too with the life of the spirit and mind. When circumstances or our choice expose these to new forces, clearly we should try to form an idea of their effect on us. Otherwise we may become seriously ill without realizing what is happening; and that is true, I would repeat, even when these forces are in the main beneficent; for every quality is haunted by a defect, and we need to watch our virtues as well as our vices.

II

LIBERTY AND REASON

CERTAINLY, whether for good or evil, in the last century a great change has taken place in the climate of our mind. I will illustrate it by two texts. The first is from the life of the poet Crabbe. 'The perfect openness of his nature . . . led him to violate occasionally what were considered, among many classes in that neighbourhood, the settled laws of clerical decorum. For example . . . he might be seen occasionally at a concert, a ball, or even a play.'[1] The second is from a review of a novel in an issue of the *Spectator* in 1949.

Ever since I encountered it in 1932, I have had a great respect for the work of Mr. —. His latest book enhances it. A woman reader, putting down this unsweetened character-study of a prostitute, observed that the essential for success in that calling appeared to be that one should not be fussy. Adriana is not at all fussy. True to type, she combines her profession with a genuine devotion to the Virgin, and reserves her love for a tiresome young student. Finally, got with child by a homicidal maniac, she encourages the dying student to believe himself the father, and feels that all considerations are satisfied by allowing his family to maintain the maniac's child. The story is redeemed from being sordid by Mr. —'s clinical exactitude, and by an irony which I like all the better for the fact that it is neither sentimental nor

[1] *The Life of George Crabbe* by his son, Chapter ix. The reference is to Crabbe's period as rector of Trowbridge, in 1814.

affected. Mr. — enjoys his story and leaves judgment to the reader.

The first of my texts shows that in the west of England in the year A.D. 1814 if a clergyman went to a ball, a concert, or, worse still, a theatre, he outraged public opinion; the second text shows that 130 years later a critic in one of the best papers of the day can write with complacency about the most tragic and degraded of human lives. (The author, if the critic is right, 'enjoys his story'.) These two extremes, one of inept taboo, one of a moral insensitiveness which is infinitely worse, a contrast between those who cannot think and those who cannot feel, show the immense chasm which has opened between us and our grandfathers. On the far side of it are human beings, with the same language, race, country, and history as our own, but, when we look below the surface, so different in their outlook that they seem hardly to belong to the same civilization. It is the profoundest of all changes, a change in a fundamental philosophy of life. That perhaps is the wrong phrase. It would be less perturbing if the critic's complacency before prostitution was part of a philosophy, the outcome of a reasoned conviction, and not the masterless drift of a ship that had lost its moorings.

Though in all actions some attitude to life, conscious or not, is implied, human beings are rarely governed by a philosophy, but rather by what the Greeks called αἰδώς, a word which we translate inadequately as 'a sense of shame'. There were, the Greeks thought, two provinces of conduct. One of these is controlled by the law of the state, which forbids the citizen to do certain things and orders him to do others. But outside this province, there is one larger and perhaps more important, where law does not interfere, and the individual is free to do what he chooses. But this province too has a master, αἰδώς, a sense of the things that 'are not done', of things that a man feels inconsistent with his self-respect or his honour, and therefore will not do though there is no one to prevent him, no penalty except the sense of shame which they bring. So, in the savage and lawless world of the Homeric poems, Achilles killed an enemy in battle but would not take his armour as spoil; 'for his soul had shame of that'.[1]

Αἰδώς, though we have no name for it, is as operative in our world as in Homer's. It is a frail, fluctuating, ill-defined force, varying from country to country and from individual to individual. But no more searching question can be asked about a people or a man, nothing throws more light on their character than this—what does their αἰδώς allow them to do and what does it forbid? It would be comparatively easy to answer this question for the age of Crabbe and to say what its public opinion allowed and disapproved. But what would be the answer for our time? If we knew it, we should have diagnosed its moral state.

Certainly the αἰδώς, the unwritten standards of our day are widely different from those of 1814. Nor is it surprising. The past century has been an age of construction but also of destruction. In the material sphere we have seen great and unbroken progress: in the sphere of ideas and

[1] Homer, *Iliad*, vi. 417.

beliefs an equally steady attrition of accepted standards, a process whose full meaning and result we cannot even yet see; and the second of these processes is even more momentous than the first, for, if it continues, it means the gradual breaking up of a philosophy of life which has been accepted in the West for 1,500 years. In consequence we live in a growing spiritual chaos which alarms us but which we seem unable to check, a mood well described in the words of a poet who lived in an age similar to our own,

> πολὺς ταραγμὸς ἔν τε τοῖς θείοις ἔνι
> κἀν τοῖς βροτείοις.

'There is a great confusion in the world of religion and of man.'[1] True, our age has its own virtues and many of the beliefs of the past survive, but they are not elements in a clear, connected, and generally accepted view of life. It is like the break-up of a frozen river: great blocks of its ice remain but they are swept along with miscellaneous flotsam and jetsam in a disordered stream, and are no longer part of a firm continuous surface over which men can walk with confidence and ease. This break-up of the philosophy of the West is the great problem of the time, on which all its lesser problems depend: for in the last resort the conduct of men is governed by their beliefs.

The two chief instruments in it were naturally beneficent forces, liberalism and science. Treitschke, no friend to liberalism, said that everything new in the nineteenth century was its work. Its purifying waters flooded up a thousand channels, cleared away the accumulated rubbish

[1] Euripides, *Iphigenia Taurica*, 572.

of centuries, and left the architects of the future free to build. In politics, in law, in education, in the social order, it attacked anachronisms and abuses, and prepared the ground for real democracy. It applied the solvent of thought to superstition, intolerance, and absurd taboos; it turned its light on ecclesiastical abuses, and forced the churches to reconsider their theology and to read their sacred books with critical eyes. It had indeed helpers—in the field of politics, the pressure of the under-privileged masses, and generally, and especially in social reform, the true spirit of Christianity, whose Founder in His day had been the champion of a rational freedom against the conventions and entrenched privilege of a ruling class. But the revolution that took place in the nineteenth century and opened an era in civilization was largely the work of this new force, which we call liberalism and which was the inspiration of 'a generation of intrepid effort to go forward'. Yet even in the hour of its triumph critical voices were raised against this great power for good, not merely by defenders of the existing order, but by those who saw and denounced the evils of the day, by men like Wordsworth, Carlyle, Newman, Ruskin; in the economic world its doctrine of unrestricted free competition is now universally abandoned; and liberalism itself today is completely eclipsed in many countries, and partially eclipsed in all. How are we to explain this strange collapse?

To answer this question we need to ask what liberalism was, and to do that we must analyse its constituents further. Though it bore a single name it combined several tendencies and forces. Of these freedom and reason are the chief; they are two of the great banners under which the world has advanced, and without which it can never advance far. The liberal believes in freedom for its own sake as giving the fullest opportunity to the human spirit, as encouraging and enabling its self-development, as alone adequate to its natural dignity and powers.

Long ago Herodotus wrote:

> The power of Athens grew; and here is evidence that liberty is a good thing. While the Athenians were despotically governed, they were not superior in war to any of their neighbours, but when they got rid of their despots, they far surpassed them. This shows that in subjection they did not exert themselves, because they were working for a master, but when they became free each individual keenly did his best on his own account.[1]

These simple words record one argument for liberalism. Set a man free and you widen the range of his mind, give scope to his capacities and stimulate him to climb to that height in human nature which is within his reach. Restrict his freedom—and some restriction is inevitable—and in so far you cramp his powers, discourage their use, and stunt his growth. But liberty is more than that. It is the recognition of the dignity of the human personality, of man as something more than an animal to be fed and housed and provided with social services, as a spiritual being who must make his own choice between good and

[1] Herodotus, v. 78. The Greek word here translated 'liberty' means the right of free speech.

evil and who grows in stature and worth by that choice rightly made; it is the recognition of him as a creature who can think, and whose virtue is to think and decide for himself. In the free state the ordinary citizen has a voice of his own, in the totalitarian state he is a mouthpiece through which others speak; in a free state he is a self-organizing, self-moving human being, in a totalitarian state he is a piece of furniture pushed about and arranged by rulers whom he has no real freedom to choose. In a free state he taxes himself, he votes for his own military service, he imposes on himself the burdens which the welfare of the community demands: in a totalitarian state he does these things at the compulsion of his rulers. Never was liberalism more needed than at this moment when we are threatened by the tyranny of the state, which may be no better, and is certainly far more difficult to shake off, than the tyranny of a church or a class.

I am considering now the ideals of liberalism; but one need only glance at the world to see that its realities are often different. Its victories have been notable; so have been its defeats. At one time or another its lights have been lit in most countries: but in how many do they burn today?

The fact is that liberty is a great gift, but also a great danger. Its value depends on the use made of it, but it gives us no guidance for its use. It is neutral: it sets men free but then leaves them to their own devices.

There are [says Ruskin] liberties and liberties. Yonder

torrent, crystal-clear, and arrow-swift, with its spray leaping into the air like white troops of fawns, is free enough. Lost, presently, amidst bankless, boundless marsh—soaking in slow shallowness, as it will, hither and thither, listless, among the poisonous reed and unresisting slime—it is free also. We may choose which liberty we like.... You will send your child, will you, into a room where a table is loaded with sweet wine and fruit—some poisoned, some not?—you will say to him, 'Choose freely, my little child! It is so good for you to have freedom of choice; it forms your character—your individuality! If you take the wrong cup, or the wrong berry, you will die before the day is over, but you will have acquired the dignity of a Free child?'[1]

There is truth as well as extravagance in these bitter words. Freedom demands a self-imposed inner discipline, based on the recognition of higher values; otherwise its army breaks down into a disorderly and impotent mob. When we ask ourselves, 'Are we free?' we need at the same time to ask, 'Have we also the firm standards and clear philosophy of life which knows how to refuse evil and choose good?' Liberalism works well or ill according to the moral quality of the citizen body. Liberty by herself cannot draw the human chariot safely. It is her nature to go in double harness; her yokefellow is law; and those who do not know the meaning and necessity of law do not long enjoy liberty.

That is true of the individual as well as of the state and Plato has given a memorable picture of the excess of liberty in the individual life. Under the title of the

[1] *Queen of the Air*, Chapter 3, pp. 143, 151.

'democratic man'—the choice of the adjective is suggestive and ominous—he describes the type that has no fixed principles or ruling philosophy of life.

When he is told that some pleasures should be sought and valued as arising from desires of a higher order, others chastised and enslaved because the desires are base, he will shut the gates of the citadel against the messengers of truth, shaking his head and declaring that one appetite is as good as another and that all must have their equal rights. . . . His life is subject to no order or restraint, and he has no wish to change an existence which he calls pleasant, free, and happy. Many a man, and many a woman too, will find in it something to envy.[1]

Such a life Plato summarizes as 'an agreeable form of anarchy with plenty of variety'.[1] It is the life without discipline, without the standards that impose a discipline. We all know the 'democratic man' and most of us have an element of him in our natures. We can buy a perfect manifestation of this 'agreeable form of anarchy' at any bookshop—those cheap newspapers which recognize no distinction between important and unimportant, and very little between evil and good, and in whose columns murders, the private life of film-stars, betting tips, and political news are mixed on no principle except perhaps that the scum tends to come to the top. Such newspapers are partly created by the public mind and partly corrupt it, and the journalism of a country is an index of its intellectual and moral state. We may be thankful that much

[1] *The Republic of Plato*, viii. 561, trans. by F. M. Cornford, p. 280 (Oxford University Press, 1941).

of our journalism (but by no means all) is free from the vices of the 'democratic man', and does not pander to them.

The 'democratic man', Plato thought, was followed by a less despicable but more formidable figure, the 'tyrannical man'. The extremes of liberty pass into despotism for psychological reasons; in the state, because however much men love freedom, in the end they love order better and need it more; in the individual, because moral and intellectual anarchy is too unnatural to be permanently tolerated at least by men with any vitality or capacity for good. Wordsworth was expressing a common feeling when he wrote

> Me this uncharter'd freedom tires;
> I feel the weight of chance desires:
> My hopes no more must change their name,
> I long for a repose that ever is the same.

Wordsworth's remedy was to put himself under the rule of the 'Stern daughter of the voice of God', of Duty. But those who are unable to find such a ruler or to discipline their own lives are apt to turn to some institution or person who will do for them what they cannot do for themselves. The growth of authoritarianism in the state or in any province of life is a symptom of liberty that does not understand the meaning of law.

The 'tyrannical man' has already appeared in several European countries, to be first the saviour, and finally the scourge, of peoples who could not discipline themselves. To us, Nazism and Fascism are simply names of evil, and

Hitler and Mussolini mere tyrants, but their original appeal was partly no doubt to nationalism but partly also to national regeneration. 'The Fascist', wrote Mussolini, 'accepts life and loves it, knowing nothing of and despising suicide: he rather conceives of life as duty and struggle and conquest, life which should be high and full, lived for oneself, but above all for others—those at hand and those who are far distant, contemporaries and those who will come after.'[1] One has only to read German novels of the twenties to appreciate the atmosphere of moral anarchy and spiritual decay then endemic in Germany from which Hitler seemed to promise liberation. His strength was that he gave a nation without belief something to believe in: he gave them a philosophy of life. That too is in part the strength of Marxism, especially outside Russia. Most people perhaps, ask from Communism not an economic system, but spiritual salvation, a creed to hold, a faith to practise, and in return for these are prepared to sacrifice their freedom. They illustrate the profound words of Pascal: 'L'esprit croit naturellement, et la volonté aime naturellement; de sorte que, faute de vrais objets, il faut qu'ils s'attachent aux faux.'[2]

That then is my first point. Liberty is essential but it is not enough. Though it strikes the fetters off the human spirit, it gives no indication what road it should follow. Yet, as Pascal says, it is the nature of man to believe and to love; but freedom by itself cannot tell him where to

[1] *The Political and Social Doctrine of Fascism.*

[2] *Pensées*, 81, edited Brunschvigg (Paris).

fix his beliefs or his affections. He must learn that elsewhere.

Freedom is one of the great forces in nineteenth-century liberalism: reason is the other. Indeed the greatest service of freedom to mankind is that it unties the hands of reason and sets her free. Once free, she breaks the fetters of prescription and prejudice, exposes superstition, fanaticism, and intolerance, and forces and helps men to see things as they are. She shows them

> The high, white star of Truth,
> There bids them gaze, and there aspire.

She 'brings things out of the dark part of our mind into the light part of it'; summons tradition and custom to the bar of her tribunal and compels them to justify their claims to respect, points out absurdities and injustices, tells us whether our conclusions follow from our premisses, and whether our conduct is consistent with our principles; she tests our ideas on the touchstone of fact.

Reason is an indispensable monitress and companion in life, but she is not a complete guide, and like other good things, she too has her defects. Kant indeed attempted to devise a practical working philosophy of life by the use of reason alone, and others have followed him in a greater or less degree. But these doctrines have been more powerful in the study than in the world. In a personality with strong, clear beliefs or at least firm habits of conduct, reason purges away the corruptions and errors of the mind. Otherwise it may be a solvent, destructive force, the 'deep plausible scepticism' of which Newman spoke as 'the development of the human reason as practically exercised by the natural man'. For it is a powerful medicine and its acids attack not only the corruptions, but also the healthy tissues of the mind. Wordsworth had this experience when, disillusioned by the later developments of the French Revolution, he turned to philosophy for help:[1] and in a later generation and a cynical mood, Browning's Bishop Blougram points out the progressive effects of scepticism.

> To such a process I discern no end,
> Clearing off one excrescence to see two;
> There's ever a next in size, now grown as big,
> That meets the knife—I cut and cut again!
> First cut the Liquefaction, what comes last
> But Fichte's clever cut at God himself?
> Experimentalize on sacred things?
> I trust nor hand nor eye nor heart nor brain
> To stop betimes: they all get drunk alike.

And why should the knife stop at God, and not proceed to operate on morals? It is easy to be agnostic about religion. But why should agnosticism end there? In fact it does not end there, as some phenomena of modern civilization show. Kipling—one of the acutest of critics, when he wished—described them more than fifty years ago in verses which contrast the innocent optimism of the Victorian Age with its critical successor, comparing the twentieth-century mind to a storm-beaten ship,

[1] See extract on p. 95f.

Threshing, crippled, with broken bridge and sail,
At a drogue of dead convictions, to hold your head to gale.
Swing round your aching search-light—'twill show no haven's peace,
Aye, blow your shrieking sirens to the deaf, grey-bearded seas.[1]

A little more of this and we arrive at a generation without either illusions or a positive faith, kept from collapse by *dead convictions*, which still influence its conduct but are no longer anchored in its beliefs. A typically modern writer, Tchekov, makes the same judgement more starkly. 'Lift the robe of our muse, and you will find an empty void. . . . We paint life as it is, but beyond that nothing at all. . . . We have neither immediate nor remote aims, and in our soul there is a great empty space. We have no politics, we do not believe in revolution, we have no God.'

I do not, of course, suggest that this mood is universal but it is common enough to make many people unhappy and ineffective, and the world a dangerous place. We have all met the character whom Romain Rolland has described—'un caracterè inconsistant qui ne croyait à rien, et une raison raisonnante, qui tranchait, fauchait, saccageait la vie, sans vouloir rien regarder'. The evil is progressive. An age of firm belief is followed by one which loses or discards its parents' creed, but keeps something of the habits of conduct in which they had been brought up. A quantum of these passes on to their children but in

[1] *The Three-Decker* (in *The Seven Seas*). A drogue, of course, is a floating sea-anchor. The italics are mine.

a diluted form and without the faith which guaranteed them. The asset wastes with each generation, and bankruptcy is the end, unless the old faith is recovered or a new one found. For, except as a safeguard against error, there is no virtue in scepticism. It is our beliefs, not our unbeliefs, that matter.

'But', it will be asked, 'if all that you have said about the liberal spirit is true, how do you explain the work of its remarkable child, nineteenth-century liberalism? If freedom gives no guidance about right conduct and if reason only throws a limited and partial light on its problems, why did liberalism do more than set men free and destroy irrationalities and injustices, why was it in the Victorian Age a great positive and creative force?' The answer, I believe, is that Victorian liberalism was much more than mere liberalism, that there were other forces in it than the spirit of freedom and the critical power of reason, other elements from which it drew content and body and driving and constructive power. Whitehead mentions them when he speaks of 'the Stoic-Christian ideal of democratic brotherhood'.[1] That perhaps is not a description of continental liberalism and it is not wholly true even of British and American liberalism, but we can discern in the latter two distinct strains. One is purely liberal, taking the word in its narrow sense; it derives from Adam Smith and Bentham and can be seen at its most characteristic in

[1] A. N. Whitehead, *Adventures of Ideas*, p. 45 (Cambridge University Press, 1946).

Cobden. But there was something more in the liberalism of Mill and Gladstone; there was an element which came from other sources and made their liberalism more than a mere belief in freedom and in reason, made it a positive and constructive as well as an emancipating force. These sources were Christianity and Hellenism.

I do not, of course, mean that Christianity and liberalism are the same thing or that Christians are necessarily liberal. I mean that in Victorian liberalism there was an element which, if not wholly derived from Christianity, was immensely fortified by it. The Christian influence can be seen even in those who rejected Christian dogma. Though they disowned its creed, they had been brought up in its atmosphere and moral teaching. Morley for instance was an agnostic, critical of Christianity, if not hostile to it, but the moralizing rhetoric of the dissenting pulpit is audible on every page of his writings. Here is his summary definition of liberalism.

> Respect for the dignity and worth of the individual is its root. It stands for pursuit of social good against class interest or dynastic interest. It stands for the subjection to human judgement of all claims of external authority. In law-making it does not neglect the higher characteristics of human nature, it attends to them first. In executive administration, mercy is counted a wise supplement to terror.

There is no sentence here, in which we do not hear the echoes of Christian ethics or Greek thought.

Of course, Morley and most of the leaders and makers of nineteenth-century liberalism in England owed even more to Greece: Mill, Grote, Gladstone, L. T. Hobhouse, Graham Wallas, T. H. Green, Henry Sidgwick, Asquith, Bryce, Lowes Dickinson, C. E. Montague, and in our day Gilbert Murray, Lord Lindsay, Ernest Barker, Alfred Zimmern—to quote only a few names—had a classical education (most of them, I may remark, in the Oxford Classical School), and there is no mistaking its profound influence on their outlook and mind. It gave their liberalism a richness and depth, which could never have been derived from Bentham or from the narrower creed of the Manchester School, which distinguishes it from the liberalism of continental countries, and which explains its influence and power. With them liberalism became not merely a political doctrine but almost a philosophy of life; and so it was protected from the weaknesses to which both liberty and reason are exposed. It had a positive philosophy which saved reason from becoming the instrument of a 'deep plausible scepticism' and liberalism from degenerating into the license of Plato's 'democratic man'. That is far less true today. In the nineteenth century, at least in Britain, the great majority of those whose outlook shaped current thought had received a classical education; and the accepted standards of the country were Christian, even when its life was not. Both these forces which infused a positive, creative element into liberalism are far weaker now, and nothing has taken their place to correct the centrifugal bias of liberty, and to compensate the destructive character of reason.

To sum up. The twentieth century is the child of

liberalism—that is, of freedom and reason. Freedom is negative; it is a condition of the good life but does not tell us what the good life is. Reason is more helpful, but she is critical rather than constructive—a guide who can only show us part of our road. It is not surprising if the child of these parents has inherited their defects as well as their virtues, if it tends to be negative and destructive—to suffer from the moral disintegration, which the extract from the *Spectator* review quoted at the beginning of this chapter illustrates, and even, in the end, paradoxically, to suffer from intellectual disintegration, a flight from reason. My conclusion is that our task is to be aware of these defects and to correct them; to recover a philosophy of life within which liberty and reason can operate freely yet safely.

III

THE NEED FOR THE STUDY OF PHILOSOPHY

Whatever the world thinks, he who hath not much meditated upon God, the human mind and the Summum Bonum, may possibly make a thriving earthworm, but will certainly make a sorry patriot and a sorry statesman.

BISHOP BERKELEY

INTELLECTUAL and spiritual disorder, and, in its train, a creeping paralysis of moral standards, as the beliefs that in the past created and supported them grow progressively weaker—so one might diagnose the sickness of our generation. It affects international relations as well as the individual life, for with the loss of its fundamental beliefs a civilization loses cohesion. Till recently a common belief, varying in detail but fundamentally the same, underpinned the peoples of Western civilization. Today they have to build their co-operation on the shifting sands of self-interest and on the remains of an historic tradition. I suggested in my last chapter that the agencies which have contributed most to our condition are rationalism and liberalism; a rationalism which destroys and does not construct and a liberalism divorced from any guiding purpose. What is the prognosis for the patient? Can we form any idea how things will develop?

We may note that our predicament is not new. It is not the first time in history that new ways of thought have shaken or shattered current views of life. Certain ages—the fifth century B.C. in Greece, the Renaissance in Europe, are obvious examples—develop an intense activity of thought, and its impact strikes violently on traditional beliefs and accepted standards and throws them into confusion. A revolution breaks out. In the intellectual and spiritual, as in the political sphere, revolutions follow the same course. At first everything is in disarray; the old order seems destroyed, the familiar landmarks disappear in the storm; 'men's hearts fail for fear and for expectation of the things which are coming on the earth'. Then gradually the storm subsides. After it things are different but the changes, however considerable, are far less fundamental than they seemed at first, for the human mind comes to terms with them and imposes its natural rhythms on life. So no doubt it will be with us. Liberty and reason, which are mainly responsible for our disorders, are in themselves wholly admirable. There is no occasion for despair; what has happened to us has happened before, and some light may be thrown on our problem by an age which had an experience closely parallel to our own. How parallel the following passages taken from its literature show.

Here is agnosticism. 'I cannot determine whether the gods do or do not exist, or what is their character: there are many obstacles to such knowledge—the obscurity of the subject and the shortness of human life.' Here is relativism. 'Man is the measure of all things.'[1] 'There

[1] Protagoras, fr. 1. 4.

are no such things as beauty and ugliness, justice and injustice: and so in general—nothing has an absolute existence: convention and habit determine human conduct: no single thing is this rather than that.'[1]

Here is a materialist theory of the universe.

Fire and water, and earth and air, owe their existence to nature or chance, and not to design; and the bodies which come next in order—earth, sun, moon, stars—have been created by means of these absolutely soulless agents, which drifted together accidentally, following their own natural laws, and produced all the heavens and their contents, and in due course, animals and plants. Neither Mind, nor God had anything to do with it: it was the work of nature and chance alone. Art, the subsequent and late-born product of these causes, herself as perishable as her creators, has since produced certain toys, with little real substance in them, such as music and painting and their companion arts. The only arts which produce anything of serious value are those which co-operate with nature, such, for example, as medicine, gymnastic and agriculture. Politics has something in common with nature, but is mainly artificial; while legislation is entirely so, and is based on assumptions which are not true. As for the Gods, they have no natural or real existence, but are artificial, conventional creations and vary from place to place, according to the convention which established them. There is no such thing as natural justice: but men are always disputing about justice and altering it; and the alterations which are made by art and by law have no basis in nature, but are valid only for the moment and at the time at which they are made.[2]

Here are power politics. 'Justice is no more than the

[1] Diog. Laert. ix. 61.   [2] Plato, *Laws*, 889 (tr. Taylor).

interests of the stronger party.'[1] 'You know and we know that the question of justice only arises between disputants equal in strength, and that the strong do what they can and the weak submit.'[2]

Laws are made by the masses who are weak, and in what their laws praise or censure they have themselves and their own interests in mind. So the attempt to get the better of the masses and keep them in their place is called injustice. But Nature herself indicates that it is just for the better and the more powerful to dominate the worse and the weak, and she shows in many ways, both in the human and in the animal world, that justice consists in the superior dominating and getting the better of the inferior.[3]

Here is pessimism. 'Nothing is certain except that birth leads to death and that life cannot escape Ruin.'[4] Here is unrestrained hedonism. 'Pleasure is good, even if it results from the most unseemly sources: even if the act is unnatural, the pleasure to which it gives rise is good and desirable.'[5] So far as their mood and content goes, these words might belong to our own epoch, though the writers are more frank and ruthless than most moderns would be; but in fact they all come from the fifth or fourth centuries B.C., and express views widely current at the time.

The disease is obviously like our own and it is due to the same cause—a sudden flaring-up of thought, the greatest in human history. Between 600 and 500 B.C. in a primitive, superstitious, ignorant world, some Greeks conceived the idea that the universe can be rationally

[1] Id., *Republic*, 338. [2] Thucydides, v. 89. [3] Plato, *Gorgias*, 483.
[4] Critias, fr. 49. [5] Diog. Laert. ii. 88 (Aristippus).

explained and understood, and there appeared among heavy surrounding clouds a patch of the clearest sky, in which one of the great lights of the human firmament, truth, shines as brightly as it has ever shone since; the spirit of science came into the world, full-grown.

As with us, its impact was first felt in the field of cosmology, with such revolutionary effect that by the middle of the fifth century B.C. Leucippus argued that the universe was composed of atoms in infinite space. From cosmology (again, as with us) reason passed to religion, morals, and politics, and there too turned the light of criticism on accepted beliefs. The formula with which it operated was the contrast between nature and convention, or what Plato calls 'Art', and some of the results can be seen in my previous quotations. Nature, it was argued, knows nothing of good and bad, or of religion, or of the laws of the state; all these are man-made, created by convention, by 'art', and with no natural authority of their own.

A society where such views are widely current might seem to be sliding into moral chaos, and indeed it is such chaos that is revealed in the famous chapters of Thucydides[1] which describe the class-war in Greece. Yet in fact Greek civilization did not founder, but lasted on, through political collapse, for another 800 years and was the foundation of the æsthetic, moral, and intellectual life, first of the kingdoms of the successors of Alexander and then of the Roman Empire.

[1] Thucydides, iii. 82 f.

The recovery was due in the first place to a young man who in later life described the Athens of the early fourth century in these terms: 'When I considered the type of men engaged in politics and the condition of the laws and of morality, the more difficult appeared the task of good government. Traditions of conduct and the observance of the law were degenerating with surprising rapidity.' These words might have been written today, and a modern philosopher might come to Plato's conclusion, that little could be done through political activity and that the remedy lay in 'surveying the question of political justice and the whole human problem from the standpoint of a true philosophy'.[1] To the working out of such a philosophy Plato devoted his life. Taking up the contrast between 'nature' and 'convention' which the materialists had used to argue that religion and morals were human figments with no basis in nature, Plato answered that the soul is as 'natural' as matter and that it, and not matter, is the original and directing force in the universe; that virtue so far from being a 'convention' is 'natural' to human beings. 'Goodness is the health, beauty, and well-being of the soul, and evil is its disease, disfigurement, and weakness';[2] and the ultimate reality in 'nature' is an eternal world beyond the senses, from which the visible world draws all its meaning and value.

The importance of Plato is not only in his doctrines but in the fact that he saw that a doctrine was necessary, and that the cure for the distempers of the time was 'to

[1] Plato, *Letters*, 325 f. [2] Id., *Republic*, 444.

survey political justice from the standpoint of a true philosophy': this involved finding such a philosophy: failing that, men would continue to walk without a guide in the perplexities and confusions of moral relativism. Plato gave to his times—and to after times—a clear principle by which men could order their conduct and judge between right and wrong. It might almost be said that he created the idea of living by principle. Certainly after his day the ancient world never lacked philosophies of life, founded on a definite intellectual basis. Within fifty years of his death the great philosophies of Greece which lasted on into the Roman Empire were in existence—Platonism in its various forms, Stoicism, Cynicism, Aristotle and the doctrines of the Peripatetic School, Epicureanism. The existence of these philosophies, dominant over the lives of men, is as characteristic of the ancient world, as the absence of equivalents for them is characteristic of our own.

My argument is that fifth-century Athens suffered from a malaise of intellectual and spiritual confusion, resembling our own and like it due to the impact of science and reason on accepted religions and moral beliefs, and that the progressive rot was stayed when Plato set himself to find a clear philosophy of life. He did not indeed establish a uniform creed for the Greek world, but he divined and initiated the way of advance. He saw that once reason has replaced the rule of use and wont, men must have a rational theory of the universe and base their conduct on it, and he thought such a theory out. Others followed his example and produced their interpretations of the world and systems of conduct founded upon them. This did not bring uniformity of belief but it did give educated men definite bases for an intelligent and rational life. After Plato, Greek thought was divided between his spiritual descendants and the materialist creeds of which Epicurus was the most famous representative, but it was free from the drift and confusion of the age of the Sophists.

We are the spiritual contemporaries of that age, but our Plato has not yet appeared. The Christian has indeed a clear philosophy of life: so has the good Marxist—he knows what to believe and how to behave, and in countries behind the Iron Curtain he is brought up to believe and behave as he should, and marches to his preconceived goal with a steady step and unwavering purpose, which the Western world envies but finds hard to emulate, living, as much of it does, on the broken meats of a view of life which it neither disbelieves nor holds with firm conviction. Things will get no better—indeed they will get worse—until we clear our minds, decide what we do believe, or at least what we are prepared to take as a working hypothesis by which to live. We might well follow the advice which Plato gave to his contemporaries.

I feel myself, and I daresay that you have the same feeling; how hard and indeed impossible is the attainment of any certainty about questions such as these in the present life. And yet I should regard a man as a coward who did not test what is said about them to the uttermost, or whose heart failed him before he had examined them on every side. He should persevere until he has achieved one of two things: either he should discover the truth about them for himself, or learn it from others: or, if this be impossible, I would have him take the best and most irrefragable of human theories, and let this be the raft upon which he sails through life—not without risk, as I admit, if he cannot find some word of God which will more surely and safely carry him.[1]

Apart from a minority, we have not yet found our certainty, or, in default of it, taken to a raft: for though we are becoming aware of the danger of drowning we have not yet considered how to avoid it. That is natural. For hundreds of years—to change my metaphor—the peoples of the West have been walking through country signposted and fenced by the precepts of a religion which they accepted. Perverse or adventurous spirits might indeed break from the road and wander where their fancy led them. But the great majority followed the beaten track, kept within the fences, and so were protected from the precipices of the difficult and broken country through which the human way leads. They had a feeling of security and—something more—an inner sense that they were on the right path. If they kept to the highroad, it would lead them safely to their destination, and if they needed more direction they could refer to the map which the Church provided. We live in a different world. The main road indeed is still there and those who follow it reach the haven where they would be. 'Adducit eos in portum desiderii

[1] Plato, *Phaedo*, 85.

eorum'. But people have broken through the fences, defaced the signposts, and questioned the accuracy of the map. The situation is changed: we can no longer live like our forefathers by use and wont, for their validity is denied. Where then shall we turn?

We should expect help from education. If it does not send out its pupils into life with at least the rudiments of a philosophy of living, it has not given them what they most need. But education has not taken this, the most important part of its duty, seriously. We have not yet fully woken up to our predicament, still less to the steps necessary to meet it; we still act as if we were living in a world supported by a common belief and accepted standards. We do not realize that we are back in the moral confusion of the Greek 'Age of the Sophists'. A good boarding-school does indeed habituate its members to certain standards, certain habits of conduct, and sometimes it imparts a definite philosophy of life: and the same is true of some day-schools. The provision in the Education Act of 1944 that 'religious instruction shall be given in every county school and in every auxiliary school' at least shows awareness of the need and makes it possible to meet it. But old habits are difficult to discard; it is easier to provide new machinery than to get it used, and the higher stages of our education suffer from a specialization which even in its own field increasingly squeezes out more general interests. In how many universities is it possible to take philosophy or religion as part of the prescribed course; in other words, in how many is there an opportunity for the student to think methodically under competent guidance about the ultimate problems of the universe and of life? But if so, what has become of the blessed word 'integration'? What are we doing to correct the fragmentation of studies which we deplore, or to prevent a university from being a mere concourse of specialisms which are hardly on speaking terms with each other? And—more important still—are our students, to whom professedly we have given the highest and completest education available, likely (so far as anything the university has done for them) to have any view of the nature of the world into which they are going or of the right way to behave in it, or even to have realized that such a view is desirable for rational living?

My suggestion therefore is that some study of either philosophy or religion or of both should be an element in any university education. It is sometimes held that the study of literature can serve this purpose and be the best road to a philosophy of life; and the reasons given for this view are that it is a criticism of life by writers of genius, that it is more intelligible and attractive to the ordinary person than philosophy, and that everyone reads it. The first two of these arguments are sounder than the last. It is a rash assumption that even university students read widely or seriously outside their special subjects. But apart from that, literature is unsuitable for this particular purpose. There are indeed poems—the *Divina Commedia*, the *Prelude*, and the *Testament of Beauty* are examples—which expound in an unsystematic way a definite philosophy of life. But literature is not in its nature rational; rather it is the expression of an infinite variety of insights and emotions. In it men of genius or high talent have recorded their feelings about life, their visions, their ideals, their passions, love and lust and hatred, hope and despair, cynicism and magnanimity. The only constant element in it is literary power, the gift of expression, a quality which sometimes, not very accurately, is called beauty. Apart from this, it is a chaos of many emotions and in reading it we are exposed to the impact of this chaos. Walt Whitman, speaking of himself, was describing literature when he wrote;

> Do I contradict myself?
> Very well then, I contradict myself,
> I am large, I contain multitudes.

Poets and novelists pour out their feelings and the air is full of these arrows, winged with imagination, these suggestions, some healthy, some harmless, some dangerous. Poets are indeed apt to see farther and to feel more deeply than most philosophers and therefore can help us to richer and profounder views; but if we are looking for anything that can be called a rational philosophy of life, we might as well try to extract it from the collection of pictures in the National Gallery as from this vast miscellany of human emotions which is called literature. If we want a rational theory of life, it is to philosophy or religion that we must turn.

It is absurd to ignore in education the religion which,

whether it is regarded as the source of truth and life, or as an *ignis fatuus* that has misled mankind, has been the greatest spiritual force in our history. Some knowledge of it is necessary, if we wish to understand Western civilization; and those who reject Christianity will find it an advantage to know more of its creed than many of them do. If we compare it in importance with some other subjects which are accepted as essentials of the curriculum, we shall be astonished—if anything in education could astonish—at the neglect with which it is treated, and at the consequent ignorance of it shown by many persons who are supposed to be educated.

But in what form are people to be introduced to it? My own belief is that the important thing—certainly the first step—is to give people an idea of Christ and of the Christian life, and if I had to teach Christianity, I should try to make two things vivid to my pupils; to make them see Christ as a person living a human life in the actual world of His day, and I should tell them that Christians believe that in the Gospels we see as much as we are ever likely to know of God, and that at any rate we see the way He behaves when He comes into the world. Then I should try to give them an idea of the early Christian communities as one gets a glimpse of these in the Acts of the Apostles and still more in the passages of St. Paul's letters, where he passes from theology to practical rebuke and advice. Here we see Christian communities in big cities, and St. Paul trying to teach men and women living in the atmosphere of the pagan world, many of them lately pagans themselves, how to behave in their own homes and in their relations to each other, what virtues to follow, what sins to avoid. I think that this might serve as an introduction to Christianity and to the Christian way of life; and it would have the advantage of being concrete, a picture of Christianity embodied in action. Afterwards would come dogma, theology, the intellectual formulations of religious belief.

We should begin, I believe, with religion, and in religion with Christianity. But only less important is the study of natural religion and natural morals, which both logically and historically are prior to revealed religion. The relation of man to the universe and the problem of his conduct in it would exist if there were no such thing as religion; and, in history, Plato and Aristotle, the Stoics and the Epicureans preceded Christ, and Christianity adopted, adapted, and enriched a rational system of ethics which it found already existing. To ignore natural religion and morals in any attempt to build up a philosophy of living is like studying medicine without a knowledge of physiology.

Something perhaps might be done to make the best of both worlds and to combine the study of religion and philosophy on the general lines suggested in the Report of the Indian University Commission (1948–9), of which I quote the relevant recommendations.[1]

'We recommend

(1) that all educational institutions start work with a few minutes for silent meditation,

[1] i. 303.

(2) that in the first year of the Degree course lives of the great religious leaders like Gautama the Buddha, Confucius, Zoroaster, Socrates, Jesus, Samkara, Rāmānuja, Madhva, Mohammed, Kabir, Nānak, Gāndhi, be taught,

(3) that in the second year some selections of a universalist character from the Scriptures of the world be studied,

(4) that in the third year, the central problems of the philosophy of religion be considered.'

These proposals have many merits. They start with religion in the concrete, in the study of those who have lived it and of the books in which its spirit is embodied, and one learns more about religion from meeting it in the flesh than from abstract arguments about it (naturally in a Christian country the emphasis here will be different from that in the Indian Report). But they go on to the philosophical approach, which is wisely deferred till the end of the university course when the student is maturer, and, having acquired some knowledge of actual religions to which the philosophy can be related, will be more aware of what he has to consider. Above all they are an attempt to attack the problem (as we have not yet attacked it) seriously and rationally; a refusal to treat the most important subject in the world as if it was indifferent; an insistence that it is the concern of all higher education.

But to return to the question of the study of philosophy for the purposes of which I have spoken. Some people argue that it is not the business of the university to provide its students with a definite view of life. That is no doubt true; but is it satisfactory that they should go out into the world without one, that they should have no rational basis for their ideas of good and bad, right and wrong, and that the university should wash its hands like Pilate and say that such matters are none of its concern? Yet does not this fairly describe the attitude of nearly all universities today? Could they not at least do something to help their students to form views of their own? That is what is wanted. It is not a question of indoctrination; the university, unless it is denominational, professes no creed except the belief in truth and knowledge. But it is, I maintain, part of its business to see that all its students get at least an opportunity of thinking about the most important of all problems, not merely in casual talks among themselves, but methodically and under intelligent guidance. This does not mean that those who teach or lecture on these subjects will or should urge any definite views on their students. Most teachers have and express definite views on their subjects, but they teach objectively, without becoming propagandists for their own theories. So it should be with religious studies; so it is already with philosophy.

I do not, of course, suppose that the study of philosophy is a panacea for our ills. Men can be brought to its waters, but they cannot be compelled to drink—to listen, to understand, and to think out a rational theory of conduct for themselves. Even when they do so, a variety of theories will emerge, not a universal creed. And when people have a theory, they do not always act upon it.

As Aristotle remarked:

No one can have the remotest chance of becoming good, unless his actions are good. But most men instead of acting rightly, take refuge in discussing virtue and fancy that they are being philosophers and that this will make them good men. They are like invalids, who listen attentively to their doctors but do not carry out any of their prescriptions. That kind of philosophy will no more produce spiritual health, than this mode of treatment will lead to physical health.[1]

And, in any case, philosophical systems, however powerfully they may influence an educated minority, leave the mass of mankind untouched. It is religion, not philosophy, that reaches and moves humanity and satisfies its needs. Yet the uses of philosophy, if different, are not less real. It clears the mind, it forces people to think, it makes them realize the importance and value of having a fixed principle by which to test and guide and strengthen conduct, and it sets them on the road of finding such a principle.

We must be clear what kind of philosophy we need for such a purpose. Naturally if we are looking for a rational theory of life, it is to moral philosophy that we should turn. But it must be a different kind of philosophy from that to which the modern world is accustomed. The subject is in bondage to the contemporary habit of specialism. Its most characteristic and most distinguished products are books and articles which only experts wish to read or are able to understand. Philosophers write for philosophers —an appreciative but small audience—and for no one else. Innocent and unconscious imitators of the devils in Milton,

[1] Aristotle, *Ethics* ii. 4, 5.

> Apart they sit retired
> In thoughts more elevate, and reason high . . .
> And find no end, in wandering mazes lost.

When they turn to ancient philosophy, they are often more interested in Plato and Aristotle than in the problems in which Plato and Aristotle were interested. Though these are justifiable activities, they do not help us—at any rate directly. But philosophy may be studied and written from a different angle, and ethical systems are or may sometimes be intended to guide intelligent men in the practical business of living. It has been so in the past. Plato and Aristotle wrote works which were at once landmarks in the history of thought and at the same time books which any intelligent man could read, and which were written—especially the *Republic*—with contemporary problems and the practical needs of men in mind. Later the Stoics and Epicureans wrote with the same end in view and the lives of innumerable Greeks and Romans show that they achieved their purpose. Among the moderns Bentham, Mill, and T. H. Green aimed at providing men with theories by which they could live. It should be possible to write a book on moral philosophy, such as the preface of Lowes Dickinson's *Meaning of Good* contemplates. 'The problems I have undertaken to discuss have an interest not only philosophic but practical; and I was ambitious to treat them in a way which might perhaps appeal to some readers who are not professed students of philosophy.' The thing has been done, can be done again, and badly needs doing.

IV

ARISTOTLE'S *ETHICS*

I HAVE been urging that we need a definite philosophy of life. What philosophy? you may ask. I will not be so presumptuous as to try and answer that question, but I will attack it indirectly.

It is surely strange that the modern world has no system of moral philosophy—I do not mean the sort of system that philosophers write and other philosophers read and nobody, at least in the world at large, thinks of acting on and living by—I mean a reasoned and methodical exposition of a practical system of conduct. It is still stranger that this should be so in an age so uncertain in its standards; yet should we look round for such a system, if only to clear and steady our minds, we shall not find one. Of course, if everyone was a Christian it would not be needed: but not everyone is a Christian: and even Christians would be no worse for having, at the back of their religious beliefs, a system of natural morals.

Now I propose to go back to a time when educated men were, in so far, better off than we are, and, giving a brief sketch of a Greek handbook on conduct, to indicate the kind of thing our age, as it seems to me, needs: though obviously our handbook would be different: it would have to take account of the modern world and its thought; and, whatever view the writer took of Christianity, he would have to take account of it. But if someone came to me and said that he was writing a textbook of ethics for the use of intelligent people, I should say to him, 'Have a look at Aristotle's *Ethics* and see if you don't find his method suggestive.' It indicates the kind of thing which, I believe, we need: it shows the sort of life which some men in the pagan world tried to live; and while it reveals points in which we have advanced farther, one can use of it the formula in which newspapers advertise a different kind of legacy. 'Persons applying here will learn of something to their advantage.'

Why Aristotle? Why not Plato? he sees more deeply and feels more intensely and he is more concerned that men should not only know the truth but that they should live by it. His view of morality is profounder, because to him morality is part of the harmony of the universe, which should also be echoed in the state and in the individual life. 'The pattern of the ideal city exists in heaven, and he who desires may behold it; and, beholding it, he will live by its laws.'[1] Nothing in Aristotle sums up so concisely the grounds of virtue. But though the *Republic* of Plato and the *Ethics* of Aristotle are both by men of genius, both deal with real problems, both are intelligible to an ordinary educated man, for our particular purpose the *Ethics* is the better. The *Republic* is the greater book but it has so much besides ethics in it—the character of the state and of society, education, art, immortality, the position of women, the usages of war, and much else. But Aristotle keeps to ethics, treats the subject with precision

[1] Plato, *Republic*, 592.

and definiteness, and supports his general theory by a detailed list of virtues with concrete illustrations of them.

And for the modern world the *Ethics* has a further advantage over the *Republic* in its approach to the problem of conduct. Aristotle was a born scientist and his greatest and most characteristic works are the writings on biology, like the *Historia Animalium*, the fruit of exact observations of the animal world, and the *Ethics* and *Politics* where he bases his conclusions on a study of human behaviour in life and society. Both in morals and in politics such an approach is badly needed at the present day. We can master Nature because in our dealings with her we use the scientific method, asking in each case what the facts are before we draw our conclusions or attempt to act. In politics we still live in a pre-scientific age and are steered on an uncertain course by a mixture of good intentions, pressure-groups, claptrap, and common sense. The time no doubt will come when here too we shall apply the scientific method, studying human nature and adapting our institutions to its facts, instead of working hand to mouth, often on untested theories and popular catchwords. The same approach is necessary if we are to have a rational and realistic system of ethics. Some day no doubt a textbook on these lines will be written and we shall have the guide to morals that we need. The difficulty is to find an Aristotle to write it. Pending its appearance we may do well to read the *Ethics* or at least that part of it—the first four books and the last—which contains the heart of its moral theory.

Aristotle was scientific in his approach to ethics. No doubt there are, as there must be in any inquiry, certain underlying presuppositions, certain principles which he assumes. He believes that there is some meaning in life, some purpose or possible purpose in human conduct, some goal or perfection which men have it in them to achieve and after which they are groping. He also believes that there is a higher and a lower element in human nature, or as he puts it, that there is something divine in men, that this is the highest thing in him and that, as far as is possible, he must live in accordance with it. These premisses he assumes. But his general method, his approach to the subject, is inductive and psychological. At the outset he rejects the Platonic idea that there exists an absolute, transcendent Good, to which our views and conduct must conform. In the true scientific way he starts from known facts, observing how men do actually behave, and then asks how far their behaviour is reasonable and to what conclusion it points. He surveys the confused stream of human life, studies the movements of its waters, and tries to determine the direction of the main current. Or, it would be a better metaphor to compare him to a grown-up, watching the half-conscious, half-instinctive cries and movements of an infant and trying to divine from them what it really wants.

What does he see? First, as he looks at us, he sees that all our actions have an aim: sometimes the activity itself is the aim—we play games normally for no further object than the pleasure of playing them; sometimes the object of the activity is a result beyond itself—we build ships in order to sail in them, we practise medicine with a view to health. But behind all or most of our pursuits and activities, there is some supreme and master aim for the sake of which we engage in them. No intelligent person makes money for the sake of making it: he makes it in order, sooner or later, to spend it; and he spends it not for the sake of spending it, but for some ulterior object which he thinks good. And so Aristotle comes to this conclusion:

If, among the ends at which our conduct aims there is one which we pursue for its own sake, whereas we pursue the other ends only for the sake of this one, it is clear that this one ultimate end will be the good, and the greatest good. Then will not a knowledge of this ultimate end be of more than theoretic interest? Will it not also have great practical importance for the conduct of life? Shall we not be more likely to attain our end if like archers we have a target before us to aim at? If this be so, an attempt must be made to ascertain, at all events in outline, what precisely this supreme good is.[1]

Thus, without an appeal to anything outside the range of common human experience, we are given a clue to a theory of right conduct. We have to discover the supreme good at which consciously or unconsciously men aim. Both ordinary and educated people in Greece described it by the word εὐδαιμονία or 'happiness'. That is the first stage in our voyage of inquiry. Ultimately the aim of all of us is 'happiness'.

But happiness is a vague term; as Aristotle remarks,

[1] Aristotle, *Ethics*, i. 2, 1 f.

different people understand different things by it; to the average man it is wealth or pleasure, to the ambitious it is honour, to others it is what Aristotle describes summarily as 'the life of contemplation', the life of the reason, in which we should include not only philosophy or science, but also art, music, and literature. So, still following the inductive method and starting from the facts, we must study these different views and decide which are the most rational. How does one decide? Aristotle's technique here may be illustrated by his criticism of the view that happiness consists in honour. He points out that honour depends on other people's attitude to us,

> whereas we dimly feel that the good must be something inherent in oneself and unalienable; and, further, that when men desire honour it is not unintelligent admiration that they want but the tribute of intelligent judges to their merits, and therefore that in their minds goodness is more valuable than mere honour and has a better claim than honour to be regarded as the end at which the life of politics aims.[1]

So he concludes that goodness and not honour is, even in the minds of the ambitious, the supreme good after which they are groping.

After his criticisms of individual views of happiness, Aristotle takes up another clue. Everything has a use or function. The eye, the hand, the foot, each has its function; a musician, a sculptor, a craftsman, each has his; and all are judged by the way in which they perform their functions; their good consists in performing them well. Is not

[1] Ibid. 5, 4.

the same thing likely to be true of man—that he, as man, has some function and that his good resides in performing it well? We must therefore ask what his peculiar function is. Then we shall know his good. It will consist in carrying out his function, in living in the fullest and truest sense as a human being.

His function does not lie in the mere fact of living, for that he shares with plants, nor in the life of the senses, for that he shares with animals. The peculiarity which distinguishes man from plants and animals is the possession of reason and its purposive use. If so, we have found what we are seeking, the supreme governing aim of man, the excellence of which he is capable and in achieving which he fulfils his nature and finds his good. As the function of, say, a pianist is to play the piano, and as his goodness, *qua* pianist, lies in playing it well, so the special function of man is the active exercise of the soul's faculties, and his goodness, *qua* man, is in exercising them well: or, to give in full Aristotle's famous definition, happiness, the supreme end of man, 'consists in the active exercise of the soul's activities in conformity with excellence or, if there are several excellences, in conformity with the best and most perfect of them.'[1] That is the general conclusion about the aim of life, to which we are led.

I have translated ψυχή by 'soul', but the Greek word has a far wider meaning than the English one and in some ways 'personality' would be a better rendering of it. The ψυχή, growing in and with the body, is, or some of its

[1] Aristotle, *Ethics*, i. 7, 4.

parts are, inseparable from it, and it is the body's reality and meaning. It is related to it as a master to a servant, as a sailor to the ship he sails. It includes both the principle of life and the powers by which we feel and act and think, the rational and moral being of man. It is akin to the nature of God and is itself divine. In its activity, aiming at excellence and in particular at the highest excellence, lies that happiness which is the natural desire and supreme end of man.

But what are these 'excellences' or 'virtues' of which we are capable and at which we should aim? They are twofold, for the soul itself is twofold and each of its aspects has an activity and virtue of its own. First there is the pure reason, whose activity consists in thought and gives birth to philosophy and science and poetry and art and music. It is 'our natural ruler and guide and, being itself divine or the nearest thing in our nature to the divine, apprehends what is noble and divine'.[1] Its pleasures are 'pure and permanent'. It is self-sufficient, for the 'wise man can practise the activities of reason by himself, though no doubt he can do this still better if he has fellow workers'. 'It aims at no result beyond itself and its pleasures are inherent in it and augment its activity.'[2] The life of reason is

> above the level of humanity; a man will pursue it not in virtue of his human nature but by the power of a divine element that is in him. If then the reason is something divine as compared with man as a whole, it follows that the life of the

[1] Ibid. x. 7, 1. [2] Ibid. 6, 8.

reason is divine in comparison with human life as a whole. So we must not listen to those who advise us, because we are men, to think human thoughts and, because we are mortal, to think the thoughts of mortality. As far as is in our power we must achieve immortality, and use every effort to guide our lives by the best element in our natures. This element may be small in size, but in potency and value it far surpasses all the other parts of a man's personality. In fact as being the ruling part and the best part, it may be thought actually to *be* the man himself. That which is best and pleasantest for any being is that which by nature specially belongs to it; and consequently the best and pleasantest life for man is the life of the reason, since the reason pre-eminently *is* the man. This life therefore will be the happiest.[1]

That then, in Aristotle's view, is the highest life for man, the life of the reason, the life of the philosopher, of the man of science, of the researcher, of the creative worker in literature, music, architecture, art; the life of Newton, Darwin, Pasteur, of Plato, Aristotle, Kant, Hegel, Whitehead, of Dante, Shakespeare, Milton, Goethe, of Beethoven and Bach, of Michael Angelo and Leonardo, of Sir Christopher Wren and Inigo Jones—the life which is being lived, though on lesser heights, by thousands of people today whose occupation is the exercise of their reason. It is a convincing view. For that kind of life does exercise and reveal something unique and very great in human nature. Man is reaching one of the heights of his being when he lives it, either as a creator in thought and literature and art, or by entering into, enjoying and

[1] Aristotle, *Ethics*, x. 7, 8.

honouring the creations of others—as we do when we enjoy art or music or literature or scientific or philosophic thought. But clearly it is a life which only a small fraction of the human race can lead; many people have not the natural endowment for it. And one sees the enormous difference and advance in Christianity which, while doing justice to the importance of reason, found something higher in a virtue of which all are capable—the virtue which St. Paul calls Love.

But to return to Aristotle. There is a side to man other than the purely rational; he has activities besides those of reason. There is the element in which our passions and appetites reside. This element is irrational but is capable of being obedient to reason, 'as a child obeys its father'—capable also of being disobedient. It has its activity and its virtues, and they constitute our moral life. These virtues of the moral life are neither natural to us nor are they contrary to nature. They are potentialities of the soul which become real and active when reason regulates our appetites, and they grow and are stabilized by habit. Virtues, Aristotle insists, depend on habits formed in accordance with the principle of right reason. We acquire moral habits by practising them, just as skills of hand or eye are acquired; as the bricklayer becomes a bricklayer by laying bricks, or a violinist becomes a master of his art by playing the violin, so we become truthful by telling the truth and brave by acting courageously, till truth and courage become second nature. And, Aristotle adds, what is true of the individual is true of the state. 'The state makes its citizens good by training them in habits of right action; this is the aim of all legislation and if it fails to achieve it the legislation is a failure: this is the way in which we distinguish a good constitution from a bad one.'[1] That is a truth sometimes forgotten by politicians.

Of all the techniques for moral education discovered by mankind, this principle of habituation is the most important and effective. It is illustrated by the child learning punctuality by coming punctually to its meals and lessons, and by the adolescent at school unconsciously learning the rudiments of citizenship by living as a member of a community. Yet goodness is not goodness if it is purely automatic. As Aristotle says, there must be an element of choice in it: we must know what we are doing and why we do it. Perhaps one may illustrate the relation of virtue to habit from golf. Success at golf largely depends on good habits—in particular on a habit of swinging in the right way. Yet a player's strokes are not automatic; there is, as Aristotle would say, an element of choice in them.

Such are the main principles of Aristotle's moral theory: that 'happiness' is the supreme aim which men consciously or unconsciously seek; that to know in what happiness consists, we must know what is the function of man; that to know his 'function' we must know his nature; that his nature has two elements, one purely rational, one non-rational but capable of being ruled by reason; that man is happy when these two elements achieve their virtue or

[1] Aristotle, *Ethics*, ii. 1, 5.

excellence, when the rational element exercises its powers in thought and allied activities, and when the non-rational element submits to the rule of reason, till from the earthy soil the virtues grow and flower. These principles, I think, are an intelligible and practical basis for a way of life.

What exactly does Aristotle mean by 'virtue'? He defines it as a quality of character which 'causes a man to perform well his function of being a man in the true sense'.[1] In other words, if we wish to satisfy the deep needs of our being, to be what we are born to be, it can only be through the practice of the virtues. In them we shall find happiness; without them we cannot find it, for in them we find our real selves.

What then is the nature of virtue? The answer is that virtue is a mean or middle state between two extremes. Thus, courage is the middle road between cowardice and rashness: liberality between extravagance and meanness, temperance between profligacy and insensibility.

You can feel either more or less than a moderate amount of fear and boldness, and of desire and anger and pity, and of pleasant or painful emotions generally; and, if you feel more or less, the feelings will be wrong. But to feel these emotions at the right time and on the right occasion and towards the right people and for the right motives and in the right manner is a middle course, and the best course; and this is the mark of goodness. And similarly there is excess and deficiency or a middle amount in the case of actions. Now it is with emotions and actions that virtue is concerned; excess and deficiency in

[1] Ibid. 6, 3.

them are wrong. It follows that virtue is a sort of middle state, in the sense that it aims at the middle.[1]

Most people probably know nothing of Aristotle's *Ethics* except this doctrine of the mean, but it is not one of his happiest theories. We must indeed admire him for having tried to define the nature of virtue at all—a task from which most other moralists have shrunk, and we can see where his theory came from. With his impulsive, passionate nature the Greek knew where his danger lay and shrank from the falsehood of extremes. Aristotle is only echoing in a philosophic form the national proverbs, 'Nothing too much', 'The half is greater than the whole', 'Sow with the hand and not with the sack'. But it is dangerous to convert a sound prudential maxim into a complete theory of morals, and the doctrine of the mean may divert the attention from the true nature of virtue, as Aristotle himself saw. He points out that it cannot be rigidly applied by any mechanical principle of measurement; the right amount of food for a miner or an athlete would be too much for a professor or a bank clerk; the amount of fearlessness or liberality or gentleness a man should show must vary according to his position and to the circumstances of the case. Further, as Aristotle remarks, 'from a moral point of view virtue is not a mean state lying between vices, but an extreme that is utterly removed from and opposed to vice'.[2] Its value lies not in the avoidance of extremes but in its own supreme

[1] Aristotle, *Ethics*, ii. 6, 10.

[2] Grant, *The Ethics of Aristotle*, i. 424.

excellence. 'Resolve a virtuous act into some quantitative law, and it seems to be rather destroyed than analysed. An act of bravery seems beautiful and noble; when we reduce this to a balance between instincts of fear and self-confidence, the glory of it is gone.'[1] Goodness is not a matter of more or less: it eludes measurement.

But Aristotle was a scientist with the scientist's instinct for precise knowledge; and he was a Greek with the Greek instinct to get things clear instead of leaving them ill defined and unexplained. So he anatomizes virtue, as in the *Poetics* he had anatomized poetry, and this is the result. The dissection in both cases is as good as can be expected: unfortunately in the process the life has disappeared from the subject on the table. Something no doubt can be learnt from the anatomy of living things, but not the whole truth about them.

So far I have been speaking of Aristotle's theory of morals, and it may seem too abstract to be of practical use. Yet we cannot escape theory, if we are to know not only what to do but why we are doing it; and my main object here is to urge that, unless it finds or recovers a rational principle for conduct, Western civilization will slide still farther down the hill. But ethics is a practical as well as a theoretical subject: its aim is action; and so Aristotle, having expounded his view of virtue, proceeds to give a list of the virtues and to illustrate them from life. This list is one of the most interesting parts of the *Ethics*, for

[1] Ibid. 210.

it is a portrait of an educated Athenian, as a fourth-century thinker conceived he should be. Some such list should form part of any work on morals that is to affect conduct. General ethical maxims may be inspiring but they are of little use for the business of living. It is no doubt well to tell an intending gardener he should aim at richness and harmony of colour, and plan a succession of bloom from spring to autumn. But he will also need detailed suggestions about the choice of plants and information about their habits and heights and flowering season. So too with morals. If an ethical system is to guide a man's life, it must be detailed and precise; it must suggest what virtues he should aim at and what they involve in practice. This the *Ethics* does.

Here is Aristotle's list of virtues. Courage, temperance or self-control, justice, are obvious choices. Liberality, the middle way between extravagance and meanness, naturally finds a place. To these are added magnificence or spending generously on great objects, spending as a gentleman should spend, a mean between niggardliness and the tasteless ostentation of the vulgar millionaire: good temper, a mean between irascibility and the lack of spirit that stomachs any insult and is incapable of indignation: amiability, a mean between obsequiousness and surliness: candour, the frank sincerity of the man who neither claims or boasts of merits which he does not possess, nor disclaims or disparages those which he has (this is Aristotle's nearest approach to the virtue of truth; but it is only a limited aspect of truth, candour in social intercourse, with which he deals): the good manners in conversation which save a man from being on the one hand boorish, dull, or offensive or on the other a buffoon. It is an odd catalogue both in what it includes and in what it omits. Humility and truth (except in a limited sense) find no place in it, and the civic virtues and a man's duty to his neighbour are not mentioned. Something must be said of these apparent omissions.

It is often held that to the Greeks humility was not a virtue; there is no word for it in their language. Yet one cannot feel that it was wanting in Socrates, who said that he had no wisdom, either small or great,[1] or in Plato who said that, compared with God, men are 'in the main puppets, though with some touch of reality about them';[2] ὕβρις, arrogance or excess in word or action, which is the opposite of humility, was in Greek eyes the greatest of sins; and Greek literature does not impress us as the work of an arrogant or even a self-satisfied people. Fundamentally, humility is a just estimate of ourselves in relation to other people and to other forces in the universe, a mean between thinking either too highly or too poorly of ourselves, between the extremes of arrogance and of false self-depreciation, which in fact are both errors of judgement.[3] Aristotle has a word for this virtue; he calls it 'truthfulness' or 'sincerity' (ἀλήθεια); and I am inclined to think that the essence of humility is covered by this 'sincerity' and by the great virtue of the sanity in mind

[1] Plato, *Apology*, 21.

[2] Id., *Laws*, 804.

[3] Aristotle, *Ethics*, iv. 7.

and conduct which saves a man from any kind of excess in action or thought or emotion. Humility became more prominent in Christian thought because of the growing sense of the surpassing greatness and goodness of God, in comparison with which man is as nothing; and that sense gave men more reason to think humbly of themselves.

The virtues which make a man a good citizen are not mentioned but that is because they are assumed. The philosopher, who held that 'the good of the State is clearly a greater and fuller aim than the good of the individual', who wrote 'A citizen who contributes nothing of value to the common stock is not held in honour',[1] and whose account of courage deals almost entirely with the courage of the citizen in war, was not indifferent to public spirit. It was essential to the life of the Greek city-state and Aristotle takes it for granted.

An omission which is more apparent than real is that of a man's duty to his neighbour. Certainly it is not emphasized and defined in Aristotle, as it is, for instance, in the Church Catechism. Yet it is clearly implied in his account of justice, of which the essence is that 'it is shown to others, and therefore thought to be the chief of the virtues, in which all virtues are included';[2] and it appears more plainly in the account of a quality whose importance is shown by the fact that Aristotle devotes a fifth of his work to it. This quality is φιλία, a word which indicates something more than friendship and something less than love. Aristotle sees in it the power which holds the state

[1] Aristotle, *Ethics*, viii. 14, 3.

[2] Ibid. v. 1, 15.

together, more even than justice. 'Statesmen seem to set more store by it than they do by justice, for to promote concord, which seems akin to friendship, is their chief aim, while faction, which is enmity, is what they are most anxious to banish. And if men are friends, there is no need of justice between them; whereas merely to be just is not enough—a feeling of friendship also is necessary. Indeed the highest form of justice seems to have an element of friendly feeling in it.'[1] To show justice and 'friendship' to one's neighbour is much the same as doing our duty to him.

And yet, having said this, we must admit that Aristotle's doctrine falls far short of the Christian ideal. In defining a man's duty to his neighbour he would hardly have gone as far as the Jewish lawyer who said that it consisted in loving him as oneself.[2] Still less, if he had been asked 'And who is my neighbour?', would he have given the answer which Christ gave in the parable of the Good Samaritan. He would have replied, 'Your neighbours are your intimates and associates, your fellow citizens, those who share your interests and ideals.' Christ's answer goes far beyond those circles, just as φιλία falls far short of the virtue of ἀγάπη which St. Paul expounds in the First Epistle to the Corinthians. It is instructive in general to note in the Epistles the virtues enjoined on the early Christians, compare them with and observe the differences of detail and emphasis in Aristotle's list.

[1] Ibid. viii. 1, 4.

[2] Luke x. 27.

We shall be less surprised at some of Aristotle's views if we remember that in the *Ethics* we have a moral system of humanism for the humanist. It is, as some of my quotations have shown, not a system which excludes religion or a belief in God, who for Aristotle was 'a living being, eternal, most good, himself unmoved, who moves the world by being its good, and therefore is the object of its desires';[1] further, it is a humanism that recognizes a 'divine' element in man and holds that his highest activities are those in which he exercises and expresses this element. Yet it is always from the human end that Aristotle approaches his problem; it is on human nature that his system is based. If he had written a catechism, it would not have contained a 'duty to God'; and the emphasis would have been on the duty which man owes to himself; on the rule by which he must live if he wishes to reach the heights of which human nature, unaided, is capable. One must not expect from the humanist a textbook for the saint.

One virtue in the list is wholly out of harmony with Christian ethics and the detailed description of it is so strange that it has even been suspected of being one of Aristotle's jokes. It is a mean between under- and overestimation of ourselves and is usually translated as high-mindedness or greatness of soul:[2] perhaps proper pride might be a better rendering, though we should consider it less proper than does Aristotle. An Englishman, and still more an American, would find the 'high-minded man'

[1] Aristotle, *Metaphysics*, xii. 7.

[2] See *Ethics*, iv. 3 f.

intolerable, and one would not suppose him likely to have been popular in Greece. A discussion of the difference between pagan and Christian ideas of virtue might be written round this virtue; but indeed the *Ethics* as a whole reveals it. Christianity has stressed the greater virtues, added to them, and often deepened them, and we might regard some of the items on Aristotle's list as nothing more than social graces. That is to rate them too low. They are the virtues of the civilized man, and in the passages of the third and fourth books of the *Ethics* where they are described we meet an educated Athenian of the fourth century.

Now, taking courage as an example, let us examine Aristotle's treatment of the virtues. A merit of his work, a reason for its being a good practical textbook of morals, is that the treatment is detailed and concrete. Charles II said that 'edifying morality is as easy as lying', but the *Ethics* are not the sort of thing that he had in mind. They do not wrap us comfortably in soothing generalities; they describe definitely what each virtue means.

The *Ethics* cannot be said to contain a complete guide to the virtue of courage, which Aristotle perversely restricts to bravery in facing death, and even then restricts still further to bravery in facing the noblest form of death, which in his view is death in battle, 'since this is the most dreadful and noble of dangers'. He says nothing about courage in facing temptation or poverty or persecution or disease or the other ills to which flesh is heir.

Aristotle takes this narrow view partly because he is criticizing Plato's view of courage—truth is apt to be a casualty in battles between scholars—partly because courage in battle was of prime concern in these small states with their citizen armies and their recurrent wars. Socrates takes a wider and truer view of courage.

> I meant to ask you, [he says to Laches] not only about the courage of the infantry but about that of the cavalry and of every other type of fighting man, and not only about courage in war, but about courage in dangers by sea, and in illness and poverty, and in political life: and not only about those who face pain or fear courageously, but about those who fight finely against desires and pleasures, standing their ground or turning on the enemy. There is this sort of courage, is there not?[1]

We should agree with Socrates. But, if for the moment we accept Aristotle's limitation of the field of courage, we shall find not only that his treatment of it is illuminating but that the principles which he lays down have a bearing on other forms of courage and on other virtues.

To some forms of fearlessness he denies the name of courage. We are not courageous if we are brave because we desire credit, or fear disgrace or—still less—punishment, or because our experience tells us that a situation is less dangerous than it seems (as, for instance, a professional soldier is less alarmed in battle than a citizen recruit, because he knows better what is happening). Nor is the

[1] Plato, *Laches*, 191 (tr. Jowett).

confidence of a sanguine temperament courage (when the optimist finds that his confidence is misplaced, he has nothing to fall back on). Nor is the fearlessness of an angry man or of a fiery or passionate nature courage. (Donkeys, says Aristotle, when hungry, are not frightened from their food by blows and adulterers are often made fearless by passion.) On the other hand the finest courage is often shown by people who are very frightened. A rational man in a dangerous situation is too intelligent not to see the danger and to realize that it may cost him life or limb.

What then, in Aristotle's view, is courage? The ardour of a passionate spirit is its natural foundation but this ardour only becomes courage when it is 'reinforced by a right purpose and motive'. This motive is the love of honour; not the honour that consists in the admiration or rewards that courage may win—for these the courageous man cares little—but honour itself, and in choosing this prize of honour, whatever the price to be paid, a man is satisfying the deepest instincts of human nature.

It is the mark of the courageous man to face dangers that would terrify any human being and are terrible to him, merely because it is honourable to face them and dishonourable not to do so. . . . Although death and wounds will be painful to the courageous man and he will undergo them with reluctance, yet he will face them because it is noble to do so and base not to do so. And the more complete the virtue he possesses and the more happy he is, the greater will be the sorrow that death will cause him; for to such a man life is of the highest value, and in dying he will know that he is losing the greatest goods, and this must be painful. But that courage is painful rather increases its value, because the brave man deliberately chooses honour in preference to the goods referred to.[1]

True courage therefore is not an impulse, but something almost in the domain of reason—a weighing of the value of life or comfort or pleasure against the value of honour.

But there is something more in it. I have translated the Greek phrase τὸ καλόν as 'honour', but it is not the honour which Hotspur coveted. Literally it means 'beauty'. We confine the word beauty to

personal appearance, landscape, literature, and art. The Greek gave it a much wider scope. He extended it to morals. Where we speak of good, he was ready to say beautiful; when we speak of evil, he was ready to say ugly. It was beautiful, καλόν in his eyes, if a citizen died for his country, if a man showed respect for religion, if a government was excellent. Victory, self-control, eloquence, frankness, wisdom, and readiness to listen to wisdom, were not merely good, they were 'beautiful'. A Greek spoke of them as if they gave him the same emotions as the sight of a beautiful human being.[2]

It is something much more than satisfaction in doing one's duty. As to the Christian mystic the knowledge of doing the will of God gives an inner satisfaction beside which suffering and death are of small account; so the best type of Greek felt a comparable delight if in some act of his

[1] Aristotle, *Ethics*, iii. 9.

[2] Sir R. Livingstone, *The Greek Genius and its Meaning to us*, p. 38 (Oxford University Press, 1915).

τὸ καλόν was embodied and became his own. Aristotle may define morality as the performance of the true function of human nature; but he holds that its reward and its moving force is the beauty which belongs to goodness. This sense of the beauty of any kind of goodness or excellence is, as I said, an unfamiliar attitude to most of us. Yet, with the belief in reason, it is one of the chief treasures in the legacy of Ancient Greece, for it adds zest and joy to life, and transforms even hardship and suffering into material for delight.

To sum up and repeat what I said at the beginning of this chapter, my object in this brief sketch of a part of the *Ethics* is not to suggest that they are a complete guide to conduct, though I think that the book contains the essential elements of a system of rational morals, but rather to draw attention to a need of our own. It is surely strange that our age has no treatise of the kind. If Wordsworth was tired by 'unchartered freedom' and felt 'the weight of chance desires', how much more parlous is our state, living in a moral chaos which presses upon us when we open any cheap newspaper and indeed in more exalted journalism and literature! My suggestion is that one of the needs of Western civilization is a modern Aristotle to write a modern *Ethics*; and that it should resemble its prototype in first establishing a theory of morals based on the relevant facts, and then describe and illustrate the actual virtues which should be its fruit. It could not give us exact prescriptions for conduct: life is too complicated for that, and in applying a principle account must be taken of the varying circumstances of each case. Yet we ought to have a principle to apply, and such a book would at least do something to clear our minds, and might bring firmer purpose and more definite principles into our conduct. But the writing of textbooks on moral philosophy is a task for master craftsmen.

V

SCIENCE

In truth 'spiritual animal' were a term for man
Nearer than 'rational' to define his genus.

R. BRIDGES

OUR age is a child of liberalism and rationalism. But it has another parent, whose influence has been even more important, is growing, and will continue to grow—science, in its pure and applied forms. In the first part of this chapter I shall use the word mainly in the restricted sense which we give it, though I regret our loss of the wider and more philosophic Greek view, to which science was the knowledge, not merely of the material and physical world but of all that concerned man. I shall say nothing of the virtues and benefits of natural science, which are obvious. Apart from its material benefits it is self-justified. 'All men by nature desire to know. . . . The feeling of wonder in men originally gave rise to philosophy and gives rise to it today; their interest was first excited by obvious problems, then advanced little by little and raised problems about the greater matters, e.g. about the phenomena of the moon and those of the sun, and about the stars and about the genesis of the universe. Since they philosophized in order to escape from ignorance, evidently they were pursuing science in order to know, and not for any utilitarian end.'[1] To be

[1] Aristotle, *Metaphysica*, 980a, 21.

indifferent to science is to disown a fundamental human instinct which calls into action the great virtues not only of the intellect but of the character. It is to refuse the inexhaustible material gifts of science, which have already added so much to the health, resources, and powers of man, and, until the internal combustion engine and atomic energy put into our hands an unlimited power of destruction, to his security.

There is little risk that we shall overlook the uses of science or our debt to it; but because we recognize them, it is possible, even more than with liberalism, to ignore the dangers and problems which it has created, and it is of these that I propose to speak. For one thing, it has upset our international relations by annihilating space. As we are so often reminded, it has abolished distance, made the five continents adjacent countries, and unified the world. At the beginning of the nineteenth century a letter took weeks, in favourable circumstances, to reach America, and its arrival was uncertain. Today we can speak from London to a friend in New York within fifteen minutes and be with him in twelve hours. We can get from the United States, from the Argentine, from the Antipodes, the food which a hundred years ago we had to grow at home, and it has become both more abundant and, in certain circumstances, more precarious. Mr. Baldwin was thought paradoxical when he said that the frontier of Britain was on the Rhine: it would be truer to say that it has disappeared. Clearly in such conditions the international relations of the past are an anachronism, and fit the body politic as ill as the clothes of a child fit a grown man. But we have not yet developed the outlook demanded by modern conditions, and we still keep the isolated, provincial mind of an earlier age to which steam and electricity were unknown. Nor is it easy to change our view. The adult immigrant into America from eastern or southern Europe, even though transplanted into a new world far from his old life and surroundings, still retains much of the outlook and habits of his past:

'Caelum, non animum, mutant qui trans mare currunt.'

How much more difficult it is for the European in Europe to detach himself from the traditions in which he has grown up and from the atmosphere which he breathes! Psychiatry on a colossal scale is needed, if we are to adapt our minds to the new political philosophy which the change wrought by natural science in our conditions demands.

Another problem created by science may be described as *embarras de richesses*. It has abolished poverty or at least has given us the power to abolish it, but this virtue has a defect which passes unnoticed. We are like *nouveaux riches*, who have come into a fortune but are too uneducated to spend it intelligently. Every capacity is a capacity for evil as well as for good, and each addition to human power is a chance to misuse it, which men are quick to seize. Take printing as an example, and put into one scale the access to wisdom, knowledge, and beauty which it has made possible, and into the other the falsehood, corruption, and rubbish which the printing-press has distributed to men: the latter scale would far outbalance the former, if good did not weigh heavier than evil. Further, the very wealth of objects and enjoyments, good and bad, useful and useless, which applied science has put at the disposal of a world that has not yet learnt to choose evil and refuse good, is a menace to true civilization. Give a small child ten shillings and take it into a well-stocked shop to spend the money, and watch it, distracted by this wealth of opportunity, take up one toy and drop it for another, and finally leave with something with which next day it will be disappointed; it does not know what it wants, still less what it ought to want. There you have a picture of many human beings in the presence of the abundance which technology has lavished on us, and a minor example of what Christ meant by the deceitfulness of riches. Needless to say, the fullest use is made of our weakness by advertisement, that peculiar development of the technological age. Its trumpet blows equally loudly the praises of the useful, the useless, the unnecessary, and the pernicious, but is mostly silent about the unnoticed treasures which are within the reach of all. It tells me that I can enjoy sunshine and natural beauty and cocktails and dancing and deck games in 'the blue Caribbean': it never reminds me that I need only look out of my window to see against the sky the dark branches of the elms, tracery more delicate and various than in any Gothic window, and, beyond, the winter sunlight suffusing the misty level of Christ Church Meadow. Why should it? The view costs nothing and there is no money to be made out of it.

Concurrently technology has impaired one of the purest enjoyments and major virtues of humanity—craftsmanship—replacing it by mass manufacture, turning the skilled worker into an automaton on the production line, making men richer in their possessions and poorer in themselves. Hence the protests of William Morris and Ruskin, who 'saw as the gravest danger to true civilization the struggle between man and the machine for mastery, whether it appears in the degradation of the operative or in the unthinking exultation in mechanical achievement'. The protests are sometimes extravagant, but the Age of Technology forgets, and needs to remember, the truth in Ruskin's words.

> No changing of place at a hundred miles an hour, nor making of stuffs a thousand yards a minute, will make us one whit stronger, happier, or wiser. There was always more in the world than men could see, walked they ever so slowly; they will see it no better for going fast. . . . As for being able to talk from place to place, that is, indeed, well and convenient; but suppose you have, originally, nothing to say! We shall be obliged at last to confess, what we should long ago have known, that the really precious things are thought and sight, not pace. It does a bullet no good to go fast; and a man, if he be truly a man, no harm to go slow; for his glory is not at all in going, but in being.[1]

These are great and formidable problems which have come wrapped up in the gifts of science. It is of course absurd to blame her; she is guiltless; it is our hands that

[1] Ruskin, *Modern Painters*, iii. 320.

are unclean. Science goes steadily about her work, revealing, as she does it, the greatness of man, and if we misuse her, the blame is ours. There is no need to be corrupted or besotted by her gifts; there is no need to employ atomic energy to destroy life instead of enriching it; and aeroplanes can be used for other purposes than bombing. The remedy is in our hands. All that we need are the firm standards and clear philosophy of life, which distinguishes evil from good, and chooses good and refuses evil.

Unfortunately our age is weaker here than any epoch in civilization since the late fifth century B.C. Its standards are not firm, its philosophy—if it can be said to have any philosophy at all—is not clear. This, as suggested in the first chapter, is partly the work of rationalism but a further destructive force has been science. It has shattered the view of the world, which, clearly held or vaguely pervasive, dominated Western civilization for centuries. New knowledge in astronomy proved that the earth is an infinitesimal fraction in the universe and not the centre of it. New knowledge in geology proved that it was not created some 5,000 years ago but has existed for millions of centuries. New knowledge in biology proved that the views of the origin of man, originating in Babylon, perhaps as far back as the twenty-second century B.C., and adopted in the Book of Genesis are—and it is not surprising—wrong. These discoveries are not as catastrophic as they appear and are still sometimes thought to be. The answer to the first was given by Thomas Hardy who watching the 'panoramic glide of the stars' reflected that 'the consciousness of such majestic speeding is derived from a tiny human frame';[1] and, earlier and more profoundly, by Pascal, who wrote, 'Le silence éternel de ces espaces infinis m'effraie', but then reflected: 'Toute notre dignité consiste en la pensée. C'est de là qu'il faut nous relever et non de l'espace et de la durée, que nous ne saurions remplir.'[2]

The true lessons from this episode in the history of human thought are that we may expect our views of the universe to change, but that these changes, if they are peripheral and not central, need not alter our fundamental beliefs, and that theology should confine itself to its own business and not undertake the work of astronomy, geology, or other branches of knowledge—pronouncements by any science on matters lying outside its own province are always rash and generally wrong. Still, in fact and for the moment, we are living in a world of shaken beliefs in which few except Christians and Communists know where they stand. When beliefs are false they must be discarded and no one can regret their disappearance. But that does not lessen the immediate crisis. This is the most difficult age in history. We have to master atomic energy; we have to see that civilization is enriched and not cheapened by the indiscriminate gifts of technology; and all the while the most difficult problems, economic, social, political, and moral are pressing for solution. This is no moment to find ourselves with broken standards and uncertain

[1] *Far from the Madding Crowd.*
[2] *Pensées*, 206, 347, edited Brunschvigg (Paris).

principles. It is ill crossing a river in flood if you are not firm on your feet.

Thus science has raised new political problems, exposed us to new temptations, and at the same time thrown our minds into confusion. Yet, though in detail its conclusions may change, there is no going back on science itself: we must go forward, and extend its empire, 'following the argument where it leads'. Any great new force that comes into the world is revolutionary; and for the moment upsets and confuses the minds of men. That was as true of Christianity as it is of science; it too was a disruptive force in the world, as its Founder warned His followers: 'I am come not to send peace but a sword. . . . I came to cast fire upon the earth.'[1] Now, as then, men have to accept the new revelation, providing against dangers that accompany it. For that, as I argued earlier in this book, we need a policy; and for an effective policy we need clear and firm beliefs.

Hitherto I have been speaking of the direct and obvious impact of natural science on the world, the political problems which it has brought above the horizon, the opportunities of misuse which its gifts allow, its disturbing effect on our traditional outlook and views of life. But more important, and much more likely to escape our notice, is its subtle indirect influence on the modern mind, the results of living in an atmosphere largely dominated by it. Great ideas run away with men, and there is no

[1] Matthew x. 34; Luke xii. 49.

trait more constant in human nature than its habit of pursuing a truth beyond its proper province: a history of civilization might almost be written in terms, first of the discovery of great truths, and then of their exaggeration. That is a danger of which the Greeks were more aware than we, as is shown by their favourite proverb 'Nothing in excess', and their inclusion of σωφροσύνη, 'balance', in the list of cardinal virtues. It can be illustrated from the history of Christianity. Dominated by the new 'good tidings' of the Gospel, many of its followers undervalued, or even rejected altogether, the gifts of secular civilization; and, later, looked in the Bible for answers to questions which science alone could solve. In what direction may science run away with us, throw us off our balance, hinder us from seeing the world with clear eyes?

It would be easier to answer these questions, if we knew better the effects on the mind of the study of different subjects, and an exact analysis of these is badly needed. What is the psychological effect of studying natural science? When we ask this question, we are apt to be dismissed with vague phrases, to be told that it gives the student a scientific attitude to life or that it trains the mind to be critical and objective. The first of these statements is vague and the second is clearly untrue. In his own field the scientist is no doubt rigidly objective: he collects the facts relevant to a problem and makes no conclusions that the facts do not justify. But, outside his subject and where his emotions are involved, he is no more objective or less liable to prejudice than the rest of us. Further the 'scientific' approach to a subject is not confined to natural science but is necessary in every field of study and habitual in any serious student. An historian would be justly annoyed if you suggested that he was unscientific; so would an economist; so would a sociologist. In any subject from chemistry to archaeology, from *kulturgeschichte* to politics the scientific method consists in ascertaining the facts and deciding what conclusions can legitimately be drawn from them. What more does the study of physics and chemistry do to discipline people in scientific method and to train them to be objective, than the study of history or economics?

We need, as I said earlier, to know more than we do about the psychological effect of different branches of study, the twist that each gives to the mind. One may think of the human mind as an eye that, for perfect sight, has to be fitted with spectacles. At birth we are unable to focus the eye either of the body or of the mind. The eye of the body quickly adapts itself to its tasks: the training of the latter is the slow and imperfect process which is called education. When it is complete, our mind, ideally, should be able to adjust itself as occasion arises to any field of vision, to the natural sciences, to history and literature, to economics, to social and political questions, to the human nature around and within us. Practically, the best we can hope for is to see more or less clearly in some of these fields and to avoid total blindness in any of them. The clearness of our sight depends partly on our natural gifts, partly on our education. If so, what corrections of our mental vision do the different subjects, by reason either of their subject-matter, or of their techniques of study, supply, and how should they be combined for the best result? If we knew the answer to that question, we could plan an ideal education. Doubtless no exact answer is possible, for each human being is individual and different from any other, and subjects differ according to the way in which they are taught. But careful and methodical analysis might in time throw some light on this fundamental problem. Meanwhile let me return to a very general consideration of the influence that we might expect the study of natural science in general to have on the mind, quite apart from the training which it gives in techniques necessary for work in physics, chemistry, biology, and the other subjects included in its province.

The method of natural science is to ascertain facts, to grasp them accurately, and to find explanations for them: and, in so far, it is a training in observation, in precision, in objectivity, and in a rational habit of mind; though these qualities may not necessarily be transferred outside its special field, and are also trained by serious study of any subject. But there is something more important still, where natural science has a special advantage. It introduces us to the material world and thereby widens immensely the horizon of the mind, extends its range, gives it a sense of infinite possibilities, and makes life more interesting and alive. It is rare to find a scientist who is pessimistic or defeatist, for he lives in an atmosphere of progress, of creation, with the promise of a heaven—at least on earth. Natural science is creative and forward-looking. The scientist is an explorer of an unknown world with infinite possibilities of discovery; and not only is the act of discovery exciting, but it leads on to action, to practical results. It seeks to know, but also to transform, the world, and this is a further excitement and stimulus to those who follow it. No other subject has these qualities to quite the same extent, though they should be present in politics and sociology, where there are immense areas waiting to be explored.

We should expect this creative, forward-looking, practical character of natural science to have a further effect on the mind. In past days I used to attend meetings of Faculties of Arts, of Science, and of Medicine, and I was struck by a certain difference of atmosphere between them. Faced with a Gordian knot, the instinct of the former was to untie it, of the latter to cut it. The 'artists' (if I may coin a word) turned a flood of criticism on the question and were concerned to get to the bottom of it and see it in all its relations and possibilities, until action was sometimes submerged in a mounting tide of doubts and difficulties. I came to the conclusion that the ideal committee would be composed, as to one-third, of 'artists', to ensure that the problem was fully analysed, and, as to two-thirds, of scientists, to ensure that something was done. A training in natural science would seem likely to foster in the mind the temper and ideal of Burke: 'To be fully persuaded, that all virtue which is impracticable is spurious; and rather to run the risk of falling into faults in a course which leads us to act with effect and energy, than to loiter out our days without blame and without use. . . . Life is a position of power and energy.'

On the other hand, a purely scientific education, uncorrected by other influences, has a narrowing effect. Natural science seems so all-embracing, that we do not notice that vast regions of life—and these the most important—do not come within its view, and a mind dominated by it would naturally be inclined to ignore or underestimate them. 'It has little to say about those creations of the human spirit which alone are immortal, great literature or great art. When we read Homer or Dante or Shakespeare, listen to a symphony of Beethoven, gaze at the Parthenon or the paintings in the Sistine Chapel, natural science has little light to throw on what we feel or why we feel it. . . . It is dumb if we ask it to explain the greatest human works or emotions or experiences,

> Exultations, agonies,
> And love, and Man's unconquerable mind.

Here we are in a mysterious yet familiar world which belongs to religion, poetry, and art, but not to science.'[1] Hence Whitehead's insistence that we should 'urge the doctrines of Science beyond their *delusive air of finality*'.[2]

The chief limitation of natural science is that it is not human. But we have to live with human beings—including

[1] Sir R. Livingstone, *Some Tasks for Education*, pp. 10 f. (Oxford University Press, Canada).

[2] A. N. Whitehead, *Adventures of Ideas*, p. 199 (Cambridge University Press, 1933). The italics are mine.

ourselves—and nearly all the problems of life are human, whereas the problems and subject-matter of physics, chemistry, and biology are not. When we enter their laboratories, we find little human there, except ourselves and our fellow workers. We are in a world of cells, elements, atoms (or whatever substitute for them the latest analysis reveals). There are obvious dangers in living in such a world. It is too unlike the world of men to be a good preparation for it: the fundamental reality in that world is human personality: the ideal society is a community of such personalities, self-controlling, self-developing, self-respecting, and respecting others. But natural science is not concerned with personality, at least in this sense and in these relations: and there is a risk that when we return to the human world, we may be inclined to ignore its difference from the laboratory, and even to treat men as if they were elements or cells. It is perhaps their training which explains why some scientists are sympathetic with Communism.

Some people turn to Communism, as others turn to the Roman Catholic Church, because it is a world religion, offers them a positive faith in an age of scepticism, makes their decisions for them, and, once accepted, relieves them of the painful task of thinking for themselves. In self-surrender they find themselves. Materialistic scientists are attracted to Communism for a different reason. Its drastic methods resemble those which they use in their laboratories with their animate and inanimate material, with atoms and cells, manipulating and controlling them in the interest of a great overriding end. It is this control and manipulation that makes the triumphs of science possible; and it seems natural to apply a similar technique to social and political problems, and so achieve more rapid and effective results than the tedious methods of persuasion allow. This technique appears to offer the quickest way to a better and more rational world, and in so good a cause it seems wrong to be too tender with individual personalities and consciences. For what is the short-lived individual in comparison with the race? That attitude, very different from the Christian belief that each individual, however stupid, however humble, has an equal value in the sight of God, is too alien from Anglo-Saxon temperament and traditions to have secured a hold in Britain or America, but it was an accepted principle in Nazi Germany and is evident in Communist Russia. No one can complain if a materialist adopts it, for it is a natural conclusion from materialist premisses.

I have suggested that an education in natural science is likely to encourage a forward-looking and active temper of mind, but that, uncorrected and unsupplemented, it gives an inadequate view of the world, and that living and dealing with atoms and cells is no preparation for living and dealing with men. All intelligent scientists are aware of these dangers, and are as anxious as anyone that science should not overweight the curriculum but be combined with humanistic studies, so that education may produce balanced human beings. All this is to the good, but, as I shall argue later, the problem is not as simple as that.

More dangerous because more subtle and less obvious is another limitation of science, an attitude to the world which, if uncorrected, induces a cramping effect on the mind, which is a widespread weakness of our civilization, but is often unnoticed.

This is an age of analysis, as any age of thought must be. Chemistry resolves matter into elements, physics resolves it into atoms (or whatever has taken the atom's place), biology resolves organic life into cells. But the method is not confined to natural science, and for the rest of this chapter I shall be thinking of science, not in the restricted sense of natural science but in this wider meaning of the term—the analytic spirit, which is characteristic of any kind of scientific inquiry in any field. When we say that the temper of modern civilization is scientific we mean not only that natural science engages a large part of its thoughts and determines much of its life, but that our civilization is scientific in the sense in which the Greeks used philosophy, that it 'loves wisdom', that in all fields it desires to seek knowledge and make knowledge its servant and its master. So literary studies employ the scientific method, so far as their subject-matter allows; a writer is 'explained' in terms of his ancestry, his early life, his education, the character of his age, the influences social, intellectual, and other, which have shaped his outlook and intellect, his subconscious mind, his Oedipus complexes and psychic traumata. Coleridge writes a great lyric of 54 lines, *Kubla Khan.* An American professor devotes a brilliant book of

600 pages to tracing the genesis and contents of the poem.[1] That is only a notable example of what in one way or another literary critics are doing in every country; and, in every field of study knowledge and understanding grow by the use of these techniques. They invade literature itself and produce the psychological novel where the skeleton and nerves of the characters are so visible that these seem animated automata and not live men and women, and we say that they have been drawn from outside and not from within. Here, as in the other instances, a penalty is paid for the increase of knowledge. Something is revealed, something is obscured; something learnt, but something lost.

May not the dominance of the analytical spirit explain why there are innumerable historical works but very little great history? The modern historian analyses events into their causes—into economic, demographic, geographic facts, into the impact of contemporary thought or the impact of individuals. He provides indispensable materials for a history that is never written. He analyses events and persons and explains them, but he fails to bring them to life. The actors in his pages are like the painted figures of historical frescoes in a Town hall or a Parliament building; we never feel them to be human beings with the same passions as ourselves. Only occasionally a writer appears who does the necessary analytic work on his subject and then so puts the results together that the

[1] J. Livingston Lowes, *The Road to Xanadu* (Constable, London, 1927).

reader is conscious not merely of parts but of a whole, not merely of dead facts but of life, not merely of an intellectual construction but of reality.

So too in the field of literature never has the general level of writing been as high as it is today and never have there been more writers—*litterarum intemperantia laboramus* as Seneca said of the first century of the Roman Empire—but there are few for whom immortality can be confidently predicted. May it not be that a mind sicklied o'er with the pale cast of thought is less likely to feel the intense and fresh impact of reality, from which great creation springs? Whether this is so or not—and speculations about genius are mere speculation—there is no doubt that the mood and atmosphere of great literature is not analytic, and in general, analysis seems alien, if not positively hostile, to great creative work. There are indeed writers of genius—Euripides, Wordsworth, Coleridge, for instance—who analyse and reflect, so to speak, before our eyes. But the analytical, reflective passages are never the greatest passages in their works. In the *Prelude* it is the scene near

> A naked pool that lay beneath the hills,

and the vision when the mist clears away on Snowdon, not the thoughts which these suggest, that are the poet's chief gift to the world. In Coleridge it is not the *Ode to Dejection*, still less *Religious Musings* that are immortal, but *The Ancient Mariner* and *Kubla Khan*. It is the same with novelists. We may enjoy and admire the intellectual subtleties of Henry James and Virginia Woolf but we recognize something far rarer and higher in *War and Peace* and *The Brothers Karamazov*, and in these the greatness lies not in the incidental reflections, which are an excrescence that would be better away, but in characters, scenes, and situations as living as life itself. Yet few men have had a more analytical mind than Tolstoy. But the gift of a great writer to the world lies not in his thoughts but in his vision: analysis and hard thinking may, and no doubt do, underlie his work but they are fused and forgotten in the hour of creation. That is why we speak of great literature as 'imaginative' or 'inspired', never as 'intellectual'.

Our civilization is increasingly built on analysis; it is the habit of mind which our higher education tends to produce, and the intellectual atmosphere which we breathe, and so its effects pass unnoticed. I am not criticizing it but pointing out its limitations; in places where its techniques are practised, a line of Wordsworth should be written up in large letters, as a warning of dangers that attend analysis,

We murder to dissect.

The parts, even if they are complete, are not the same as the whole. Dissolved into atoms, the solid world is no longer itself. Reduced to cells or to an amalgam of psychological impulses, human beings 'no more *make* that Whole which commands our devotion, than some shredded dissection of human tatters *is* that warm and breathing beauty of flesh which our hearts found delightful'.[1] Analyse a thing and the life leaves it, but life is the most important thing in the world, and analysis not only does not help us to see it, but it encourages us—so potent and interesting and engrossing is it—to forget the existence of what it cannot reveal.

I remember the impression produced on my mind when, as an undergraduate, I read a famous work of literary analysis, Aristotle's *Poetics*. Here was a brilliant and illuminating account of literature, of poetic diction, of tragedy—its function, its structure, of the place in it of plot and character, of the nature of the ideal tragic hero; but there was not a word in it of poetry as I understood it. I had been given a critique which I could apply to *King Lear* or to any great drama; if I used it, I could judge them better. But I was not helped to appreciate them, if appreciation means not accurate dissection but a sense of their greatness, of that impact which a masterpiece, as a whole, makes on the imagination. Aristotle apparently was not interested in that. The *Poetics* is a great piece of analytical criticism but you could read it without learning what poetry is.

To describe what is missing in analysis I have been using phrases such as life, reality, imagination, sense of the whole. What is at the bottom of this distinction? What is the difference between poetry as it is seen in a great work of analysis like Aristotle's *Poetics*, and in poetry itself? What do we miss if we analyse perfectly a

[1] F. H. Bradley, *Appearance and Reality* (Oxford University Press, 1930).

poem, an historical event, a human character, a flower, a piece of music, a work of art, and stop there, resting content in our analysis? At bottom this is a metaphysical question for philosophers to answer, but one can at least see certain facts. Mere analysis, however exact and complete, misses something and that the most important thing. There is a double road to truth, the road of analysis and what we may call the road of intuition, and the first road only takes us part of the way. We have to see that Shakespeare is a great poet and Michael Angelo a great sculptor, the Parthenon a great building; we have to see that St. Paul's words about love in the 13th chapter of the First Epistle to the Corinthians are true. No amount of argument or analysis will prove these things, unless we perceive them and perceive them to be so. No analysis of the technique embodied in the Parthenon, no talk of entasis or asymmetry will help us. And if someone says that Shakespeare is inferior to Shaw or Michael Angelo to Henry Moore, or the Parthenon to the London University building, or love to efficiency or to knowledge, there is no way of convincing him or proving that he is wrong. 'Questions of ends', said Bertrand Russell, 'are not amenable to rational argument', and the same is true of the most important things in life. The road that leads to reality is the road of vision. The penalty of not using the road is to miss reality.

Two great writers, who combined analytical with imaginative genius, have spoken of the danger to which the analytical mind is exposed. It is the subject of a poem by Ibsen, which portrays the thinker under the image of a miner;[1]

> Beetling rock with roar and smoke
> Break before my hammer-stroke!
> Deeper I must thrust and lower,
> Till I hear the ring of ore.

There you have the analytical thinker digging deeper and deeper into his subject. But in the end

> I lost the sense of light
> In the poring womb of night;
> Woodland songs, when earth rejoiced her,
> Breathed not down my hollow cloister.

In less enigmatic words Ruskin expresses the same loss of 'the sense of light' when he describes the mood that came upon him after minute study of the details of Gothic architecture in Venice. 'I went through so much hard dry, mechanical toil there that I quite lost the charm of the place. Analysis is an abominable business. I am quite sure that people who work out subjects thoroughly are disagreeable wretches. One only feels as one should, when one doesn't know much of the matter . . . I lost all *feeling* of Venice.'[2]

But we need not go to Ruskin and Ibsen to learn about the dangers which attend the analytical habit of mind. Every school illustrates them. 'In the garden of Eden Adam saw the animals before he named them: in the traditional system [of education] the children name the

[1] *Lyrics and Poems from Ibsen* (tr. Garrett), pp. 20 f.
[2] John Ruskin, *Praeterita*, ii. 366.

animals before they see them.'[1] The pupil masters a text-book on botany, but may never have seen a flower in the sense that Wordsworth saw a daisy or Bridges saw a sea poppy or Tennyson saw the 'flower in the crannied wall'; they may remain unaware of its beauty and mystery. As Whitehead says, 'When you understand all about the sun, and all about the atmosphere, and all about the radiation of the earth, you may still miss the radiance of the sunset.'[2] Yet of these two forms of knowledge, both real, the second is the more profound. It belongs to what Whitehead calls 'the deeper intuitions of the human spirit'.

Analysis deludes us into thinking that we know all about things whose inner reality we miss. It was said of an eminent statesman that his weakness was a tendency to suppose that an analysis of a problem was the same thing as a solution of it. It may be said of the modern world that it is apt to suppose an analysis of something to be identical with knowledge of it, whereas it is only a step to real knowledge. The habit of analysis accustoms us to be content with a view of the world which seems complete and is not.

But it has another danger. Uncorrected, it actually weakens the habit of mind which gives a fuller and farther vision. It contributes to our materialism by destroying our sense of wonder. Σέβας μ' ἔχει εἰσορόωντα is a recurring

[1] A. N. Whitehead, *Science and the Modern World*, p. 285 (Cambridge University Press, 1925).

[2] Ibid., p. 248.

phrase in Homer, 'Wonder possesses me as I see...'. There speaks the poet, and the man to whom this wonder comes most often, who feels thus most intensely about the greatest number of human experiences, is the man who sees and knows most of the universe. But it is just this sense in which we are apt to be deficient. Awe, reverence, mystery (except in connexion with a crime) are not words characteristic of our time. Ruskin said: 'the tree of knowledge is not the tree of life': 'we live to contemplate, enjoy, act, adore, and we may know all that there is to be known without being able to do any of these'.[1] Our age understands knowledge and action; it regards contemplation as a waste of time; it has a narrow view of enjoyment; and adoration means little to it. The highest powers in man are a trinity—knowledge, love, and worship: strong in the first, we are weakest in the last two of these. The spirit of analysis, uncorrected, fosters our weakness and impoverishes the mind; it has 'explained' all things or is on the way to 'explain' them, and their mystery withers away. We forget that the mystery has merely been pushed back beyond the range of our short sight and remains at the heart of things.

> An idle poet here and there,
>   Looks round him, but for all the rest
> The world, unfathomably fair,
>   Is duller than a witling's jest.

We live among marvels and never notice them.

Uneasy stirrings reveal the disquiet of the human spirit

[1] Ruskin, *Praeterita*, ii. 336.

with conditions in which it cannot rest, and of such stirrings there have been many in recent years. Instincts suppressed, needs unsatisfied, always make themselves felt and a reaction against the purely analytic spirit of the age appears in many forms. It can be seen in Nietzsche's later writings, in Bergson's philosophy of the *élan vital*, in the theology of Kierkegaard and Karl Barth, in existentialism, in the thought—if it can be called 'thought'— of D. H. Lawrence, in surrealism. To it we should attribute an irrationalism which has been more aggressive and clamant in this rational age than in any other epoch in history, and which in politics is illustrated by Hitler and the Nazi philosophy. We are too annoyed by these violent winds which disturb the intellectual atmosphere to ask where they take their rise and we dismiss them as irrational—as indeed they are. But there is more to them than that. Like romantic movements in literature—and in a sense they can be called romantic—they warn us of something deficient and incomplete in our outlook; and they contain an element which human nature needs. D. H. Lawrence writes,

> To me, chaos doesn't matter so much as abstract, which is mechanical, order. To me it is life to feel the white ideas and the 'oneness' crumbling into a thousand pieces, and all sorts of wonder coming through. I know there has to be a return to the older vision of life. But not for the sake of unison. And not done from the *will*. It needs some welling up of religious sources that have been shut down in us: a great *yielding*, rather than an act of will: a yielding to the darker, older

unknown, and a reconciliation. Nothing bossy. Yet the natural mystery of power.[1]

The cries of Lawrence are incoherent, but he had some reason for protesting: there is a truth after which he and others are groping. Our task is to accept what is true in these movements of the mind and to reject what is false; to remain rational and yet to be aware of a world beyond reason.

In my next chapter I shall say something more about the analytical spirit, its uses, and the dangers that attend its excess, and make some suggestions about avoiding them.

[1] D. H. Lawrence, *Letters*, p. 605, edited Aldous Huxley, (Heinemann, London, 1932).

VI

SCIENCE (*continued*)

My own criticism of our traditional educational methods is that they are far too much occupied with intellectual analysis.

WHITEHEAD

I SUGGESTED in the preceding chapter that the analytical, scientific approach gives an incomplete, and in some ways a distorted, view of the world. Is then nothing gained by analysis? Should we be better without it? Certainly not. One obvious reason is that our civilization largely depends on analytical techniques, and without them would cease to progress, and probably collapse. Indeed, in some fields we need more analysis: in politics, for instance, where we operate with very difficult words, like democracy and liberty, without, for the most part, analysing or attaching any clear meaning to them. If everyone who uttered them was liable to pay five shillings, unless he could define them intelligently, the state would draw a respectable revenue from the fines. But, apart from the need of clearing our minds on these ideas and giving some definiteness to hazy catchwords, we need a realistic study of 'political man': we ought to analyse much more exactly the actual conditions of politics and to study closely in relation to these the characteristics of the human material out of which the state is composed—its intellectual capacity, its ways of thinking, feeling, and behaving—so that we can adjust our political machinery accordingly. A naval architect builds a vessel with close regard to the materials at his command; the ship of state is constructed with little attention to the ability of the human material to take the stresses to which it is exposed: yet it has to face worse weather than Atlantic storms. A more exact analysis of this human material would make the ship more seaworthy, provided that it did not lead us to regard politics as a mere matter of mechanism, or to forget the larger visions of ideal possibilities, which beckon the world on to unscaled heights. No doubt in time the anthropologists and sociologists will help us here, but their influence is as yet hardly felt in politics.

But, quite apart from these practical considerations, the analytic, rationalizing spirit protects humanity against one of its greatest dangers. In its absence we should relapse into the superstition and ignorance from which it has done much to free us. We can see in Hitler and in D. H. Lawrence what happens when reason loses control. I spoke of two roads of knowledge, that of analysis and and that of intuition or imagination. The road of imagination is a dangerous road, for the country of irrationalism lies about it. Though reason without vision is short-sighted, vision without reason is apt to take phantoms for realities and dreams for truth, and we should gain nothing by escaping from the death-in-life of mere analysis to the life-in-death of surrealism. Reason, thought, analysis, fortify the mind against fantasies and discipline it against insubordination. At the moment we suffer more from the spirit of analysis, but irrationalism is always waiting for its opportunity; and, since any excess tends to reaction, in an over-intellectualized age men are often tempted to a flight from reason.

Even in fields such as literature, art, and music, where analysis might seem out of place, it is important. Behind the greatest artistic and imaginative creations of man lies an immense amount of intellectual activity, absorbed and incorporated in the finished work, as years of experience are incorporated in the wisdom of a wise man. The Parthenon and Santa Sophia were the creations of patient labour of thought as well as of intense imagination. In the background of all great poetry, except, in some cases, lyric, we detect the workings of a powerful and disciplined mind which has sifted and tested the materials with which it builds the cloud-capp'd towers, the solemn temples, of genius; and the more fully we know what has gone into the completed work, the more we shall understand it, the more we shall find to appreciate. Analyse the mind of Hamlet, his temperament, his feeling for his father, the shock of the Ghost's supernatural monitions, his position as heir to the throne, the danger in which he stands, the impact on him of his mother's conduct and his uncle's crime, of the treachery of his 'good friends' Rosencrantz and Guildenstern, of his relations with Ophelia and her death—clearly there is far more to move us than if we read the play casually and without thought. Only, having made our analysis, we must escape from the analytical mood, cross the line from the world of thought into the world of feeling, let the work of genius which we have been dissecting into parts become a whole again and *feel its immediate impact*—not on our intellect, but on our spirit.

In the last chapter I quoted Ibsen and Ruskin on the effect of analysis on our power to feel, Ibsen on the loss of 'the sense of light' which accompanies it, and Ruskin on the way in which, while studying the details of Gothic architecture in Venice, he 'lost all *feeling* of Venice'. I will now cite two further witnesses, a philosopher and a poet, one from our own time and one from the last century, who speak of the same phenomenon and throw more light on it.

There are two great philosophic poems in English, *The Prelude* and *The Testament of Beauty*. Both are works of thought, feeling, and insight. Bridges's poem is the fruit of scholarly and cloistered meditation,

> The harvest of a quiet eye,
> That sleeps and broods o'er its own heart;

in the *Prelude* we hear the echoes of an intense and stormy personal experience. Wordsworth, in time more remote, is in other ways closer to us, for, like us, he lived through a revolution that shook Europe. Those who think of him only as a tranquil, meditative writer who

> Laid us as we lay at birth
> On the cool flowery lap of earth,

may be surprised to find in him, more than in any other

English writer, more even than in Byron and Shelley, the generous ardour of a generation which saw in the French Revolution a movement destined to end ancient wrong and to inaugurate a new democratic world.[1]

> Bliss was it in that dawn to be alive,
> But to be young was very heaven.

The Wordsworth, who, when war broke out between England and France, exulted in English defeats, sat silent when prayers for victory were offered up, gloomily watched the English fleet in the Solent prepared for 'that unworthy service' of war with France[2] and 'fed on the day of vengeance yet to come', is a surprising figure but the real man. The Reign of Terror brought him dismay, the fall of Robespierre revived his hope, the imperialism of Napoleon completed his disillusionment, and Wordsworth looked for consolation in philosophy and embraced Godwin's *System of Political Justice*. Disappointed by the world of action, he turned to the world of analytical thought. It is his description of this experience and its sequel, which occupies the last four books of the *Prelude* and which contains Wordsworth's final view of life, that is instructive to us.

For a time he found relief and renewed hope in these analytical studies, but this did not last.

> So I fared,
> Dragging all precepts, judgments, maxims, creeds,
> Like culprits to the bar; calling the mind,
> Suspiciously, to establish in plain day

[1] See *Prelude*, ix, x, xi.

[2] Ibid. x. 283 ff., 316.

Her titles and her honours; now believing,
Now disbelieving; endlessly perplexed
With impulse, motive, right and wrong, the ground
Of obligation, what the rule and whence
The sanction; till, demanding formal *proof*,
And seeking it in everything, I lost
All feeling of conviction, and, in fine,
Sick, wearied out with contrarieties,
Yielded up moral questions in despair.[1]

Nor was it merely that he 'found no end, in wandering mazes lost'. It was not only certainty that was missing. He was conscious of living in an incomplete world and found that 'the love of sitting thus in judgment'[2] interrupted his 'deeper judgments', and 'cut off his heart from all the sources of her former strength'[3] and from

Those mysteries of being which have made,
And shall continue evermore to make,
Of the whole human race one brotherhood.[4]

Such was the effect of his devotion to 'Reason's naked self', to the analytical and purely intellectual approach to truth.

Where was the road of escape? Wordsworth found it, not by deserting reason, but by reinforcing her with faculties without which she is always shortsighted and sometimes blind. He describes this power of the spirit by different terms, speaking of 'sweet counsels between head and heart', 'intellectual power, fostering love', 'a feeling intellect',

[1] *Prelude*, xi. 293 ff.
[2] Ibid. xii. 121 f.
[3] Ibid. 80.
[4] Ibid. 85 f.

Imagination, which, in truth,
Is but another name for absolute power
And clearest insight, amplitude of mind,
And Reason in her most exalted mood.[1]

Nowhere, it will be noted, throughout the *Prelude* is reason renounced; rather she is amplified and enriched, her vision takes a wider range, her nature is deepened, and warmed by generous sympathies. Wordsworth recovered his power of 'worshipping among the depths of things', and again

In Nature's presence stood, . . .
A sensitive being, a *creative* soul.[2]

He did not lose the gifts of reason but used them less narrowly.

Again I took the intellectual eye
For my instructor, studious more to see
Great truths, than touch and handle little ones.
Knowledge was given accordingly; my trust
Became more firm in feelings that had stood
The test of such a trial; clearer far
My sense of excellence—of right and wrong:
The promise of the present time retired
Into its true proportion; sanguine schemes,
Ambitious projects, pleased me less; I sought
For present good in life's familiar face,
And built thereon my hopes of good to come.[3]

De nobis fabula narratur.

This is the language and outlook of a poet, recording a personal experience. The greatest of modern philosophers

[1] Ibid. xiv. 189. [2] Ibid. xii. 206. [3] Ibid. xiii. 52 f.

sees in the contemporary world the same disease as that from which Wordsworth suffered, and traces it to the dominance of the analytical habit in our education. In *Science and the Modern World* Whitehead criticizes the modern mind for 'its contraction of concrete apprehension: the whole is lost in one of its aspects. . . . My own criticism of our traditional educational methods is that they are far too much occupied with intellectual analysis.' Instead we 'should aim at eliciting our concrete apprehensions'. 'What we want is to draw out habits of æsthetic appreciation.' 'In regard to the æsthetic needs of civilized society the reactions of science have so far been unfortunate. Its materialistic basis has directed attention to *things* as opposed to *values*.'[1] In our pursuit of truth, which is the aim of science, we risk missing beauty, which is the aim of the universe. 'In itself . . . there seems to be no special importance about the truth-relation.' To say this is not to deny that truth is essential. Its 'general importance for the promotion of Beauty is overwhelming. . . . There is a blunt force about Truth, which . . . is akin to cleanliness—namely to the removal of dirt, which is unwanted irrelevance. . . . Falsehood is corrosive.' But the besetting danger of a scientific, analytic age is not to realize that beauty is 'a wider, and more fundamental, notion than Truth'.[2]

[1] pp. 246 f., 252. The word 'æsthetic' is used in the widest sense, indicated in the following words: 'The habit of art is the habit of enjoying vivid values.'

[2] A. N. Whitehead, *Adventures of Ideas*, 341 ff. (Cambridge University Press, 1933).

So Whitehead diagnoses the disease; it is interesting to note his prescription for its cure. We are apt, when we are aware of our weakness, to blame specialization for it and to demand that the humanists should study more science and the scientists read more literature and history: all this is to the good, but, as Whitehead said, it is no real remedy. He is not afraid of specialization. 'The student should concentrate within a limited field. . . . I should be inclined even to increase the facilities for concentration rather than to diminish them.' But the narrowness which such concentration encourages cannot be counteracted merely by including science, literature, history, art, and other subjects in the specialist's education. These no doubt will find a place there, but they may be, and often are, mere patches of plaster loosely attached to the surface of the mind. It is not a question of acquiring new knowledge but of correcting the eye of the soul. The important thing is to develop in the specialist a seeing, aware, wide-ranging habit of mind. 'The centre of gravity of the other side of training should lie in intuition without an analytical divorce from the total environment. Its object is immediate apprehension with the minimum of eviscerating analysis. The type of generality, which above all is wanted, is the appreciation of variety of value.'

Both these words, 'value' and 'variety', are important. Values are various: they are not confined to religion, to human relations, to literature, music, and art. They are indeed more obvious in these, more difficult to overlook, but they are latent in all the pursuits and activities of man (including, of course, science) which without them are cold and dead. No education is adequate unless it awakes the sense of value, in its various incarnations, unless it achieves a balance between the analytic intellect and something higher, and reveals the existence of realities beyond criticism, analysis, and even understanding; this is the sphere of the higher life of men.

How, practically, is this to be done? We have to develop 'the appreciation of variety of value'; and the word 'variety' is almost as important as the word 'value'. For though it is disastrous to have no sense of values, and so to miss the life in things, it is dangerous to have limited values, however genuine they are, for this is to do injustice to the richness of experience and to take the part for the whole. 'Things fall apart; the centre cannot hold.' Scholarship that is narrowed into technique; art whose ideal is art for art's sake; a scientific education which neglects the humanities; a literary education indifferent to science; all these are liable to the Pharisaism, which is proud of its virtues, unaware of its limitations, and certainly lacks 'the appreciation of *variety* of value'. The remedy is, not to dole out snippets of history, literature, art, and science, but to develop a mind sensitive to values and aware of their infinite variety.

Here our education is defective: it lays too exclusive a stress on analysis: one of the stock injunctions to teachers is 'Teach the pupil to think, give him a critical mind.' That no doubt is an essential element in education and, observing the banquet of claptrap, misrepresentation, and half truth which at general elections some party politicians serve up to the British electorate, I do not wish to underestimate its importance. But to teach people to see and feel is more important still. By overstressing the critical attitude we may produce characters—they are not uncommon—both superficial and satisfied with their superficiality. They turn a keen eye on men and things, they can pull them to pieces, but they see them in parts and not as wholes, and they concentrate on their weaknesses. (A good example of this is Lytton Strachey's *Eminent Victorians.*) And though they learn to be critical, they are apt never to learn the most effective and penetrating method of criticism—that which consists in such intimacy with excellence, that anything less than the excellent dismisses itself and needs no inspection to disclose its defects. The best way to make a person critical is to show him the first-rate till anything inferior ceases to attract. That is in fact the way in which we learn—if we ever learn it at all—to distinguish good from bad not only in literature, art, or music but also in human nature—not by observing the defects in inferior specimens of them but by becoming familiar with their great masters.

A proper training in this kind makes a man quick to perceive any defect or ugliness in art or in nature. Such deformity will rightly disgust him. Approving all that is lovely, he will welcome it home with joy into his soul and, nourished thereby, grow into a man of a noble spirit. All that is ugly and disgraceful he will rightly condemn and detest while he is still too young to understand the reason; and when reason comes, he will greet her as a friend with whom his education has made him long familiar.[1]

To the injunction, 'Teach your pupil to think', I should like to add a further injunction, 'Teach your pupil to see and feel.' The soul has two eyes and both need developing fully; if either is shortsighted, the vision is imperfect. There is the critical, analytical eye which measures and assesses and protects men from illusions and delusions. But there is also the eye which enables them to contemplate, enjoy, and adore. In our age concentration on minute and microscopic study often impairs its vision, and we live, contented with our myopia, in a world unrealized because the organ which could see it is neglected and atrophied. We are like one-eyed people, congratulating themselves on the vision of their single eye. But in everyone the poet should keep company with the rationalist: then we have the highest type of educated man. In our age and education the rationalist is apt to crowd the poet out, and in consequence we unconsciously lose the power of discerning realities which must be taken into account if our philosophy of life is to be adequate to the facts.

So our task is first to find the studies which will bring the spirit into touch with values, and develop the habits of mind which analysis does not develop, and then to pursue these studies in the way which will develop them. Some subjects lend themselves more easily to analysis and so tend to draw the mind in that direction: others are

[1] Plato, *Republic*, 401.

more richly charged with values. Pre-eminent among such subjects are art, music, poetry—not that these are the only subjects which will serve our purpose, but that in them we are compelled to feel rather than to think, to be receptive rather than critical, if they are to mean anything to us; and therefore they stimulate and develop our power of feeling which Wordsworth calls the 'creative soul'. Indeed the recent development of art and music and drama in education may be regarded as an attempt, sometimes unconscious rather than deliberate, to satisfy a human instinct which hitherto has been starved. In none of the subjects is the effect more obvious than in art, not in the old-fashioned formal 'drawing lesson', but in the creative work now familiar in any school. One has only to look at the specimens pinned to the wall at any prize-day exhibition, to divine the processes that have gone to their making. These paintings, however rudimentary, are the creation of feeling: the pupil's whole nature has gone out in an effort to seize the subject, to penetrate to its heart.

This is the mood, the approach to life, of the poet—the mood of which Keats speaks. 'A poet . . . has no identity—he is continually informing and filling some other body. . . . When I am in a room with people, if ever I am free from speculating on creations of my own brain, then, not myself goes home to myself, but the identity of everyone in the room begins to press upon me, so that I am in a very little time annihilated.' And again: 'If a sparrow comes before my window, I take part in its existence and pick about the gravel'; and again: 'I feel more and more every day, as my imagination strengthens, that I do not live in this world alone but in a thousand worlds. No sooner am I alone than shapes of epic greatness are stationed around me, and serve my Spirit the office which is equivalent to a King's body guard—then "tragedy with scepter'd pall, comes sweeping by". According to my state of mind I am with Achilles shouting in the Trenches, or with Theocritus in the Vales of Sicily.'[1] This power of laying the mind open to impressions needs to be developed where it is absent and kept alive where it exists: for unless men are poets as well as rationalists, they will have little worth while to reason about.

I do not, of course, suggest that art, music, or poetry can give us a philosophy of life. My point is that they can correct the eye of the mind by exercising, and so developing, certain capacities of vision in it, which analysis leaves undeveloped; and that thereby they enable us to become aware of realities, on which the reason can reflect, and on the basis of which it can construct a philosophy; but that if we miss or ignore these realities, we shall have a very inadequate idea of the world, and lack the necessary material for a philosophy of life.

I have spoken as if art, music, and poetry were the best media for our purpose. But, of course, it can be achieved through any subject (among them, through natural science): nothing in the world is pure prose, though in some

[1] *Letters*, edited by M. Buxton Forman, pp. 69, 228, 241 (Oxford University Press, 2nd ed., 1947).

things the poetry runs in thinner veins or lies a little deeper below the surface. On the other hand, any subject, however rich in imaginative quality, can be so treated as to lose its effect. Let me take literature to illustrate my meaning and consider what, in teaching it, we should do and what we should avoid, if it is to call to life and feed the receptive, feeling and imaginative powers of the mind.

First, obviously, we must approach it from the angle of imagination, not of thought or analysis. A thorough study of *King Lear*, for instance, will involve consideration of its date and sources, of the differences in the text of the quarto and folio editions, of the characters, of the meaning of rare words and obscure phrases. But when we wish the play to stir the imagination, all such things must be ignored or left in the background of the mind, and we must read it as Shakespeare felt and wrote the story, as it was first played on 26 December 1606 at Whitehall, as it is acted today—as the story of events in the lives of certain men and women. We can forget everything else but we must see them come alive, human beings of like nature with ourselves, and we must become absorbed in their emotions and experiences. And so too with whatever literature we read, drama, epic, lyric, poetry, or history.

Second, we must forget the idea of being examined in it. Examinations are the curse of education; there are practical reasons why we cannot dispense with them; they may serve to concentrate the mind and make knowledge precise; they may be convenient tests of industry or ability; they may apply to the pupil the spur to work which a good teacher does not need. But they have the same relation to real education as the promise of rewards has to good conduct: they may stimulate it, but at the same time they corrupt it. And of course you cannot examine on great literature: you cannot set questions on sublimity and beauty, on the human agonies and heroisms of great tragedy: and if you try, you will get from the schoolboy or the undergraduate answers which either are not worth reading or which have been borrowed from some book of criticism. We can test our pupils' knowledge of the subject-matter and language by examination, but in doing this it is not on *King Lear* that we are examining them, and there is a danger that we may leave them with the impression that these subsidiary problems and scholarly interests of ours are the play. What is true of *King Lear* is true of all great literature, indeed of anything that is literature at all.

Third, if we wish to arouse and feed the imagination, it should be done through *great* literature, which shakes our dispositions with thoughts beyond the reaches of our souls. For this purpose we should read Homer rather than Apollonius Rhodius, *Paradise Lost* rather than the *Idylls of the King*, Shakespeare rather than Shaw, Thucydides or Gibbon or Macaulay rather than some modern history textbook which leaves us accurately informed but uninspired. Perhaps I may here quote in illustration an experience of my own. I was taught at school to read French and German. In French we read *Tartarin sur les*

Alpes and a novel of Dumas, *Le Capitaine Pamphile*, which presumably were chosen as likely to amuse us, as possibly they did; but I can remember nothing of them except their titles. Our German teacher followed more drastic and unorthodox methods, which no doubt would be condemned on correct principles of pedagogy. After a year of *Easy German Passages for Translation* we were plunged—when we could hardly swim—into Schiller, Heine's *Lieder*, and Goethe's *Faust*. We struggled with them, our heads frequently under water, and the master who taught us was not a great teacher. But, at least in *Faust*, and to a lesser degree in Heine, we met great literature, and it remains as an unforgettable memory and an imperishable possession. We might have read Daudet and Dumas till we had got them by heart, but they would never have stirred the imagination or left anything valuable behind.

But a difficulty remains. Some of the greatest literature needs—especially at school and even in the university—interpretation of its greatness: it is possible to read *Hamlet* and notice little in it but a ghost and some murders, to read *Paradise Lost* and to wonder why the experts admire it so much. But can we find enough interpreters? Some teachers are incapable of conveying to their pupils the quality of great literature, and would make themselves and the literature seem ridiculous if they tried. The immediate reaction of schoolboys to such attempts is rarely sympathetic. So our well-meaning efforts to stir their imagination may fail completely, and it may seem better to abandon great works of imagination and fall back on Daudet or Shaw, who at any rate are lively and amusing, and are writing about a world we know. This is a real, practical difficulty. How is it to be surmounted?

One can only give a partial answer: to the end of time education will be frustrated by our weaknesses as teachers. On the other hand great literature does of itself often make an impact on the mind. Archbishop Lang tells of a young thief in Portsmouth who read the Bible in prison because it was the only book allowed him, and who said, ' "When I read them names, like Nebuchadnezzar, Chedorlaomer, Nebuzaradan, Belteshazzar and them others, I shut me eyes and I seem to see great shapes movin' before me." Great shapes—symbols of great empires rising and falling in that old world: and this guttersnipe had the imagination to see them.'[1] That is an instance of the power of a great book to stir, crudely no doubt, an untaught mind.

Literature has still more of this power when it is not merely read but learnt by heart, and this is an argument for a practice of which there is too little in modern education. At the moment of learning them the words of a great poet may have little effect on us, but, stored in the mind, they ripen there, and, long after we learnt them, come to life, and 'pierce us, as if we had never before known them, with their sad earnestness and vivid exactness'. When Mr. Churchill was presented with the Free-

[1] *Cosmo Gordon Lang* by J. G. L. Lockhart, p. 122 (Hodder and Stoughton, London, 1949).

dom of Brighton he began his reply by recalling his schooldays in that town. It was there, he said, that

I began to learn by heart many of those passages of poetry which have been a great treasure and comfort to me during my life—heroic poetry and famous tales and legends of the past. The committing of passages to heart, and the recording of them, is the most valuable part of education and sinks more deeply into the composition of the child than a lot of chatter-patter that is hurriedly spread over him in order to pass some examination.

Hence too the value of drama in education, provided that the plays chosen are really great. (From the point of view of education—perhaps from any point of view—to act second- or third-rate plays is useless.) Learnt by heart and acted, great drama is absorbed by the mind and becomes one of those unconscious influences which mould thought and feeling and personality. A man, whose career has not lain in the fields of scholarship, once told me that the greatest educational influence of his life was acting as a boy in the *Agamemnon* of Aeschylus at Bradfield.

For the purpose of awakening and strengthening the power of imagination, it is on poetry, art, and music that we must chiefly rely. It is difficult to say which is most effective. Art is the most creative. The child starts from something seen, but at once passes from sight to vision, and moves into a world of its own making, trying either directly to represent what it sees or to penetrate and express its inner nature. The effort calls out all its powers of sight and insight, and, incidentally, reveals its personality better perhaps than any other test can do.[1] But there are limitations to the educational power of art. In it the child expresses itself, but it cannot rise above the natural level of its capacities, though it may develop them to their farthest stretch. Here great music and poetry have an advantage. They take us outside and beyond ourselves: so far as our nature allows, we see the world through the eyes of great men, and, lifted for a moment on the shoulders of genius, catch glimpses of things beyond our natural powers of vision.

If we have to discriminate still farther and choose between poetry and music, poetry seems to me better for our purpose. The young can hear great music but to get the intimate experience of it which comes from playing Beethoven or Bach is beyond the powers of all but a few, whereas they can not only read but act great drama. And poetry in general has the further advantage that it is more directly related to the actual world than music. Its themes are mostly ordinary things or people; the more exotic or abnormal poetry is, the less great it is. But to the poet ordinary things are not ordinary—it is almost a definition of poetry that it sees nothing common on the earth—and he communicates his vision to us. It is a vision of the world we know, but that world is changed. We see in it more than our unaided eyes would see.

Here is an example of its operation. Imagine a man on Christmas Eve standing on a hill—it may have been that ridge above Oxford which looks out over the Vale of

[1] See Herbert Read's *Education through Art* (Faber, London, 1943).

the White Horse—and listening to the sound of church-bells. Nothing could be more ordinary: the experience might happen to anyone. But when it happens to a poet, it ceases to be ordinary.

A frosty Christmas Eve
  when the stars were shining
Fared I forth alone
  where westward falls the hill,
And from many a village
  in the water'd valley
Distant music reach'd me,
  peals of bells aringing:
The constellated sounds
  ran sprinkling on earth's floor
As the dark vault above
  with stars was spangled o'er.

Then sped my thought to keep
  that first Christmas of all
When the shepherds watching
  by their folds ere the dawn
Heard music in the fields
  and marveling could not tell
Whether it were angels
  or the bright stars singing.

Now blessed be the tow'rs
  that crown England so fair
That stand up strong in prayer
  unto God for our souls!
Blessed be their founders
  (said I) an' our country folk

Who are ringing for Christ
  in the belfries to-night
With arms lifted to clutch
  the rattling ropes that race
Into the dark above
  and the mad romping din.

But to me heard afar
  it was starry music
Angels' song, comforting
  as the comfort of Christ
When he spake tenderly
  to his sorrowful flock:
The old words[1] came to me
  by the riches of time
Mellow'd and transfigured
  as I stood on the hill
Heark'ning in the aspect
  of th' eternal silence.[2]

When we read this poem, we too share the experience of Robert Bridges and follow his mind as it moves to and fro, from the scene to the thoughts which the scene evokes—from the sound of the bells and its sensuous effect (the bright sounds scattered over the earth as the bright stars are scattered across the sky) to the thought of the first Christmas, and then to the thought of the power of country churches in English life; from the scene in the belfries to the meaning which the music suggests

[1] Presumably 'I will not leave you comfortless, I will come to you' (John xiv. 18).

[2] 'Noel: Christmas Eve, 1913' from *October and other poems* (Oxford University Press, 1931).

to the hearer. Nothing, I repeat, could be more ordinary than the subject; anyone might stand on a hill and listen to church bells on Christmas Eve: and with most of us that is all there would be to it. But when it happens to a poet, a commonplace scene is transfigured, as though a sudden shaft of sunlight had fallen on a featureless landscape, and our minds and lives are enriched by the vision. No detail is falsified; there is no tampering with the facts from which the poem is born. They are unchanged, but they have become significant. That is an example of the quality and uses of imaginative power, without which men cannot enter regions even more important and more real than those revealed by thought—a power which certainly needs cultivation.

In his *Defence of Poetry* Shelley wrote

We have more moral, political, and historical wisdom than we know how to reduce into practice; we have more scientific and economical knowledge than can be accommodated to the just distribution of the produce which it multiplies. The poetry in these systems of thought is concealed by the accumulation of facts and calculating processes. There is no want of knowledge respecting what is wisest and best in morals, government, and political economy, or at least, what is wiser and better than what men now practise and endure. But we let '*I dare not* wait upon *I would*, like the poor cat in the adage'. We want the creative faculty to imagine that which we know; we want the generous impulse to act that which we imagine; we want the poetry of life: our calculations have outrun conception; we have eaten more than we can digest. The cultivation of those sciences which have enlarged the limits of the empire of man over the external world, has, for want of the poetical faculty, proportionally circumscribed those of the internal world; and man, having enslaved the elements, remains himself a slave.

If these words were true in 1821, how much truer are they when 'our calculations have outrun conception' still farther, and the mood of analysis still more dominates our spirit.

PRINTED IN
GREAT BRITAIN
AT THE
UNIVERSITY PRESS
OXFORD
BY
CHARLES BATEY
PRINTER
TO THE
UNIVERSITY